Also by Elizabeth Kendall

WHERE SHE DANCED:
THE BIRTH OF AMERICAN ART-DANCE

THE RUNAWAY BRIDE:
HOLLYWOOD ROMANTIC
COMEDY OF THE
1930'S

AMERICAN DAUGHTER

RANDOM HOUSE NEW YORK

AMERICAN DAUGHTER

Discovering My Mother

ELIZABETH KENDALL

All rights reserved under International and
Pan-American Copyright Conventions. Published
in the United States by Random House, Inc.,
New York, and simultaneously in Canada by Random House
of Canada Limited, Toronto.

RANDOM HOUSE and colophon are registered
trademarks of Random House, Inc.

Grateful acknowledgment is made to Farrar, Straus & Giroux LLC for
permission to reprint "Prayer to My Mother" from *Poems* by Pier Paolo
Pasolini, translated by Norman MacAfee. Translation copyright © 1982
by Norman MacAfee. Reprinted by permission of Farrar, Straus
& Giroux LLC.

Library of Congress Cataloging-in-Publication Data

Kendall, Elizabeth.
    American daughter: discovering my mother / Elizabeth Kendall.
        p.   cm.
    ISBN 0-679-45292-3
    1. Mothers and daughters.   I. Title.
HQ755.85.K45   2000
306.874'3—dc21   99-39912

Random House website address: www.atrandom.com

Printed in the United States of America on acid-free paper

9 8 7 6 5 4 3 2

First Edition

Book Design by Barbara M. Bachman

PRAYER TO MY MOTHER • PIER PAOLO PASOLINI

It's so hard to say in a son's words
what I'm so little like in my heart.

Only you in all the world know what my
heart always held, before any other love.

So, I must tell you something terrible to know:
From within your kindness my anguish grew.

You're irreplaceable. And because you are,
the life you gave me is condemned to loneliness.

And I don't want to be alone. I have an infinite
hunger for love, love of bodies without souls.

For the soul is inside you, it is you, but
you're my mother and your love's my slavery:

My childhood I lived a slave to this lofty
incurable sense of an immense obligation.

It was the only way to feel life,
the unique form, sole color; now, it's over.

We survive, in the confusion
of a life reborn outside reason.

I pray you, oh, I pray: Don't die.
I'm here, alone, with you, in a future April . . .

translated from the Italian by Norman MacAfee
and Luciano Martinengo

A LONE BLUE CAR WITH SUITCASES STRAPPED ON top is heading south on Highway 61, the two-lane highway that cuts north and south through the low, flat fields of southern Missouri. It is raining and the sky is dark gray. Seen from above, the road is shiny as a canal; the car seems to be skating straight down it. A gas station with a turquoise canopy comes into view on the opposite side of the road. The car slows, crosses the highway, and pulls in by the gas pumps. The right passenger door opens. A young woman gets out and lifts her face to the rain as the attendant puts the gas nozzle into the car's tank. The woman jumps up and down in place. The attendant removes the nozzle and replaces it in the gas pump. The young woman circles around the car's front and gets in on the driver's side. The car heads off again, picking up speed down the slick highway.

At the bottom of the picture, the glimmer of a creek appears at right angles to the highway, flowing under a low bridge, and beyond that comes a big gray hauling truck, heading up the road on the other side, toward the blue car. The truck crosses the creek, passes the little car in a spume of water, then roars up out of the picture. The blue car, as if shaken, whips back and forth on the road, then plunges into the low wall of the bridge. The car eats up the wall; they become one mangled shape. The suitcases slide off the car roof into the creek. Silence. Stillness. Rain in a flat landscape.

A back door of the crushed car inches open. A grown boy edges out of it, stumbles to the side of the road, and waves his arms. A dark green car appears down the road and pulls over; its driver gets out and confers with the boy. From the other back door of the wrecked blue car a blond girl emerges, then two more boys, one grown, one small. Finally the young woman edges from the driver's door. The children lean against the blue car, or take small steps by the side of the road as more passing cars pull over and stop. People get out, surround the children, cluster around the blue car, peer into its open doors.

A police car comes from the bottom of the picture, flashing blue lights, and pulls up next to the other cars, followed by a long black van sounding a siren. From the black van, attendants run with a stretcher to the blue car. They bend into the front passenger seat. People from the other cars usher the children over to the black van and help them through its side doors. At the blue car, the attendants lift from the passenger seat the inert form of a woman, put her on the stretcher, and load her into the black van. The van, with siren sounding, sweeps out across the road and heads back the way the blue car was going. The leftover people swirl about the scene for a few minutes; then they get into their cars and drive away.

THIS ACCIDENT HAPPENED in 1969, on April 3, at about 10:30 in the morning. I was the person in the driver's seat. The children were my brothers and sisters. My mother was the dead woman they pulled from the passenger seat.

I know now that such an event comes without warning. It is not caused by anything except the rain, the truck's splash, the jam of brakes, the panic of the blinded driver—me—on the flooded road. It isn't the result of emotions that have been building in a family, or in a person.

Except that, when people tell themselves their own stories, they usually arrange the telling so that things lead into other things. The very practice of laying down facts, of choosing to put certain events next to others, implies a sequence of cause and effect. Sequences of cause and effect are almost impossible to rub out from any narrative.

Here were a young mother and a nearly grown daughter—I was the oldest of my mother's six children. She and I were assumed by almost everyone to be alike. We often switched places in the same task, the way we traded off the driving that day. We confused each other about where one of us started and the other ended.

What does it mean, looking back at the shapes of both our lives, that one of us caused the other's death? Given the conditions of that road, which had seen many accidents and was later rerouted, it could have been she who was driving, and I who died, though she might not have been driving as fast as I was. I can't imagine how she would have lived after that. But I am the one left alive.

I don't believe in special fates or appointed lifetimes; a skeptical nature was implanted in me at birth. But if I tell the story, there have to be sequences, buildups of meaning, an unfolding design. A few years ago, when I was in my mid-forties, the confluence of an anguished love affair and the undeniable fact of aging signaled that now was the moment to go back and find the design of events that had led, however blindly, to that fatal moment of violence on a Missouri road. I took out my mother's diaries, her calendars, her notes on her projects. I began calling up my father, my brothers and sisters and aunts, and my mother's friends—the different friends from the different parts of her life—and my own friends from childhood. The past, that many-layered existence of the family that was smashed in a moment, started to rise up and show its buried face. And the guilt that had lived underground in me, holding deep parts of me in the grip of numbness, began to loosen and give way in the light of remembering.

Demeter, the Greek goddess of grain, lost her beloved daughter, Persephone, down a crack in the earth that led to the underworld. That myth has always seemed miraculous to me because of the passion it describes between a mother and a daughter. That passion has been a real and abiding force in my life, both before my mother's death and after it.

Of course my story has the wrong person dying. But the effect of the grief is the same. Bereft, Demeter wandered the earth until she found that place again where Persephone had disappeared, and she could pick up her trail.

AMERICAN
DAUGHTER

I WAS A PRODUCT OF OKINAWA, OR RATHER, A REFLEC-
tion of Okinawa in my mother's young heart. Jud, her beloved
older brother, was killed by a Japanese sniper on that lettuce-
green and bloody island in late April 1945. She was a sophomore
at Vassar College, up the Hudson River from New York City.
"Today is my nineteenth birthday," wrote Betty, née Elizabeth, in
her diary on April 30, "and three hours ago Daddy called me from
St. Louis to say that Juddy was killed. It still hasn't sunk in," she
continued, "so all my friends think I am being the most wonderful sport in the world."

The friends were Pooh and Coe and Buff and Mare and Non-
nie and Lyd. The girls at Vassar in those years tended to have nick-
names that also suited dogs. Since their brothers, their neighbors,
their real or potential lovers (those shadowy figures who would
hand them their futures) were all fighting on the Front, anything

unsportsmanlike was unbecoming. Their job was to keep the home fires burning. Notwithstanding such sacred duties, Betty burst into tears in chapel on V-E Day, May 8, when they sang "As he died to make men holy, let us die to make men free!" At this moment, Julia Ward Howe's words, with their grand clumping together of Christianity and Americana, passed into the core of my mother's personality.

The unusual thing about my mother was that while she was earnest and moral, she was also strikingly pretty. She wore her hair long, in a brown pageboy to her shoulders with a barrette holding the finger waves on the left side. She had a generous mouth, a turned-up nose, the look of an expectant, if slightly didactic child. Because of sports, she had a slim, thoroughbred figure, which was clothed, while she was at Vassar, in collegiate sweaters and pleated skirts and shiny new saddle shoes with socks. Even when she dressed up, in her Tyrolean-style black velvet suit and pumps, she looked to most people like a picture of health, like a glass of milk, like America itself—like Rita Hayworth, if someone were to remove the hurt and fright and incipient numbness from Rita Hayworth's eyes and replace it with intense sincerity. To the other Vassar girls, however, my mother was a pure midwesterner. While impeccably coed on the surface, she was missing the suavity of the New York or Boston girls. There was something eerily fresh about her and her irrepressible fund of "Oh, goshes." You could say my mother embodied that curious mixture of humility and hubris in the air of her native city of St. Louis, Missouri.

In the days of river travel and the fur trade, St. Louis had been the queen city on the American frontier, alive with frontier scouts and settlers and shopkeepers busily making their fortunes from the exploration of the great West beyond. Then, in the mid-nineteenth century, the coming of railroads and the invention of the steel plow had edged the newer, brasher Chicago into the limelight. Markets fled north, and St. Louis began its long, nearly imperceptible slide into second place, cultivating, as it went, a compensatory vision of a more delicate, more nuanced city essence. With almost its entire modern history bound up in decline, the city in its upper echelons became a place of Byzantine exclusivity. It was controlled, from the Gilded Age on, by a clique of businessmen referred to, variously, as "the Big Cinch" or the "West End crowd" (after the enclave of urban palaces where they lived). The finest hour of the Big Cinch was that spectacle to end all spectacles: the St. Louis World's Fair of 1904, with its airy pavilions, its fountains of colored water, its fabulous midway featuring Egyptian cooch dancers, its catchy waltz tune "Meet me in St. Louie, Louie. . . ."

But the Big Cinch lived on beyond the Fair, conducting both private and public business through an interlocking structure of clubs and secret societies. Thanks to the lingering influence of St. Louis's French founders and the presence of a cultivated German business elite, these clubs and societies gave off a more cosmopolitan aura than other such organizations in midwestern cities. The wives and daughters of the Big Cinch, such as my grandmothers and great-grandmothers, were exposed to a more serious brand of culture than was available to society patronesses in the other cities. Along with the sense of superiority, there lingered, however, even in the hearts of the best St. Louisans, the suspicion that somewhere in the East, or in the South, or in Europe, lay real gentility—that their homegrown version was only a sham.

By the twenties the city's mix of social exclusivity and cultural longing had produced two women poets of note, Sara Teasdale and Marianne Moore, not to speak of that male seeker of pure tradition, T. S. Eliot. The city had produced as well a host of lesser characters who, in the teens, twenties, and thirties, flaunted their eccentricities in the boarding schools and colleges of the East. Some colorful St. Louisans were still circulating in the East when my mother came of age in the forties. But in the city itself, the migration of the elite to the suburbs, and the ideological simplifications of wartime, had weakened the fabric of cultural life. Girlhood in my mother's time was missing even a hint of the world-weariness that had belonged to the flappers of her mother's generation. For the college-age Betty Conant in 1945, a determined good cheer wrapped in an aura of innocence was the order of the day.

It didn't help the innocence that, before his death, Jud had been writing a stream of loyal, sensitive, almost maternal letters home to his parents and four younger sisters, letters in which he made it clear that the small web of St. Louis social connections and interlocking "good families" and houses and schools and dances and the normal frivolous doings of adolescence had become sacred to him as he slogged through the war in the Pacific. "Tell that sister of mine at Vassar," he wrote in his last letter of March 20, from somewhere in the South Pacific, "that she had better get that idea of a job out of her head and finish her schooling and attend to preparing herself to run a family and not a business firm, for the boys are going to want to marry real true honest to goodness *old-fashion* girls when they get back and not some scientific, over hypothetical masterminds. It is the *old fashion* girl who will win out when we get back . . ."

At Christmas 1945, when the boys who had survived came home, so did the college girls, and there was much fox-trotting in homes and country clubs. Uncle Garneau and Aunt Etta, godparents with cigarette drawls, gave Betty a debutante party at the country club to which they all belonged, down the road from the Conants' house. The vast green tract of the St. Louis Country Club lay at the center of the new and exclusive suburb of Ladue. Because St. Louis occupied the west side of the wide Mississippi River—across it, to the east, lay Illinois—the city's suburban expansion could fan out only in a westerly direction. In 1914 the city fathers who were club members had bought this piece of land due west of downtown, then molded its hills and creeks and old ivy-covered trees into a Scottish-style golf course, in the middle of which they planted a Mediterranean-flavored clubhouse of white stucco, arched doorways, and black shutters.

On the night of Betty's party, that clubhouse was decked with Christmas greenery and ablaze with light, as in the good old days before the war. Car after car drove up to its low entrance, from which orchestra music wafted. Across the red-tiled floor the receiving line could be glimpsed, where Betty stood in her ivory satin gown, flanked on one side by her dark-haired, dark-gowned mother, Biff, and on the other by her balding, diminutive, tuxedo-and-tailed father, Sam, the real host of the party.

Sam Conant was the second and golden son of old T. P. Conant, self-made dynamo of Sligo Steel & Industrial Supplies, which sold machine tools of all sizes. Sam had gone to Princeton, roomed next door to F. Scott Fitzgerald, cavorted in Fitzgerald's famous Triangle Club show *The Evil Eye* (cross-dressing as one of the smaller chorines—a "pony," in the term of the day), learned to smoke a pipe and play really excellent golf, shipped out as an officer to France in World War I, came home to St. Louis and married, in 1922, in the "winter marriage of the season," a quiet and prudish dark-haired beauty, Elizabeth "Biff" Bemis.

Biff Bemis had a religious side—Sam had met her in church. She loved music and played the piano. She was also a member, albeit a modest one, of something bigger than Sligo Steel: the dynasty of the brown paper bag. Bemis Brothers Bags was begun in the mid-nineteenth century as a maker of jute sacks for the raw cotton coming up the Mississippi on the riverboats. The two original brothers found they could sew those sacks on machines faster than the Negro slaves could sew them by hand. From jute sacks, their sons and grandsons expanded to muslin sacks, then to paper bags, and set up factories in nineteen places around North America.

Sam Conant got a seat on the Brothers' board when he joined the family, as a sideline to his work at Sligo Steel. In a marriage of contretemps and misunderstandings, Sam and Biff had produced first sturdy Jud, then smart, earnest Betty, then Dodie (Helen), Gigi (Louise), and Janey (Jane), at the time sixteen, nine, and seven. Grieving separately and bitterly over their son, Sam and Biff put on their bravest faces for their eldest daughter's party. Betty, as she had promised her diary, did her best to "keep lively" for them.

But something happened at the party to upset everyone's expectations. A tall young man in Marine green, twenty-three years old, with jet-black hair, a classic profile, and flying medals pinned to his chest, kept appearing at my mother's side. He cut in on her dancing partners, he brought her glasses of champagne, he sat by her on couches while she rested from dancing. Henry Kendall wasn't exactly a stranger; he was the son of neighbors who lived in the same manicured subdivision as the Conants—the Kendalls at 35 Briarcliffe, the Conants at 25. He had gone to high school with Jud Conant. Now home from the Pacific, he had been assigned to take Betty's Vassar houseguest to the party. He had driven to the house in his family's Ford, been admitted to the downstairs hall, and seen my mother in her ivory gown at the top of the stairs. That one look had propelled him into action.

It wasn't just how she looked that fired his imagination, Henry told Betty that night, it was his own eerie connection with her brother's death. Eight months before, Henry and his fellow Marine pilots had flown their Corsairs off an aircraft carrier to the just-cleared Yungten Airfield on Okinawa, had dug their foxholes in the mud and begun the lookout for hidden "Jap" soldiers. By a trick of fate, the day Henry arrived in Okinawa was the day Jud Conant died. Having heard about that death in a letter from his mother, who was always up on society doings, Henry went down alone to see the grave in Okinawa's makeshift cemetery, a field of crude white crosses—thousands of them—sloping down from the western side of the airfield to the Pacific, with Jud's cross somewhere in the middle. He said a prayer.

Henry's parents were not quite as illustrious as the Conants. Arthur Kendall, though a Harvard man, hadn't been born in St. Louis, but had come from Boston in 1916 with a letter of introduction to Crunden Martin, the manufacturing firm he now commanded. (It made galvanized tubs and jobbed paper products.) Thirty years in the business community had advanced the family on the local front. Henry had gone to Country Day, the best boys' school, then started Bowdoin College in Maine only to leave after two years for flight training in Pensacola. But full social glory had eluded the family, or so his mother believed, and her younger son had dutifully absorbed her longing. When he saw Betty at the top of the stairs, he saw not just a pretty girl but a social paragon. "She will be my wife," he said to himself in a sort of fever.

While Betty had been eagerly attentive all around, she now seemed transfixed by the near stranger who had appeared in the uniform her brother would have come home in. The unpreparedness of these two wartime youths, her unplumbed grief and his slumbering passions—the very vagueness of both their natures, kept in shadow by the country's obsessive gaze into the blue sky of the Pacific arena—focused on a single point. A plan. A script. He pressed, she gave way. For him she would quell any doubts, impel the decisions, fill up the empty space between dreaming about the future and beginning to do something, anything at all, in the jittery climate of postwar America.

It was something of a mismatch. Betty was an idealist, a musician, and just barely a woman—she had gotten her first period late, the year before, at eighteen. In her childhood she had played the piano on radio broadcasts. As a teenager she had vowed to go to nursing school, but in college she had flirted with a grander role in a larger arena. Just before that 1945 Christmas break, she had come up with the idea that Vassar should take a lead in the movement for world government, "in view of the atomic bomb." "Why shouldn't the students be the ones to wake up first? (like the German students in 1848, my history paper!)," she asked her diary. Might she herself be the one to sway the whole college at a mass meeting?

If Betty was transparent with moral fervor, Henry, by contrast, was politely opaque, with an ironic edge almost undetectable in public. Kept in strict check by his tall and imposing mother, who had piloted the family's social ship around Depression shoals, Henry had developed a drawling, parent-pleasing social manner. He also had a secret, inarticulate life that revolved around birds. He had kept small birds in his room since he was a silent five-year-old, falcons since he was an undersized twelve. His wildest dreams were embodied, in an inchoate way, in the sport of falconry, where ancient pedigrees, Darwinian cruelty, and manly stoicism mingled with the call of the wild. His bird proclivities, though, were not visible at that December party. There he was simply Arthur and Rebecca's stunningly handsome son, home from the war and headed for Harvard on the GI Bill. He shook hands with Sam Conant. He complimented Mrs. Conant on her younger daughters, whom he'd seen at the house. And he hovered darkly and ardently about my flustered mother.

Dick Thomas from Yale Law School had once put his arm around Betty in the backseat of a convertible on a double date. "That was probably pretty bad," she wrote in her diary, "but it started because it was cold as heck in the backseat with the top down." Which boys were "sincere" and really in love with her, which ones were "wolves" and "handing her a line"—that was hard to tell. But Henry persisted. He borrowed a small plane from Lambert Field—Marine pilots could do that—and performed stunts above the Conants' house. When they both went east to college in the spring of 1946, Henry came down from Harvard to the Vassar dances. He whispered to Betty and kissed her forehead on the dance floor. He took her up for airplane rides (and let her vomit in his hat). Back at Harvard he wrote her daily letters and periodically woke up the whole Vassar dormitory with his long-distance calls.

They were secretly engaged in February. In March Henry sent some snapshots home to 25 and 35 of a weekend in the country, in which a laughing Betty rode him piggyback. Number 25 erupted in grim warnings and dire predictions. Sam Conant made a hurried trip east. The engagement was announced at a Vassar dance, and marriage followed in July, a marriage meant to protect the two young people from each other, or rather, to protect their families from possible disgrace. He'd just turned twenty-four; she was twenty.

I FLARED INTO being right under the wire—on their wedding night at the Park Plaza Hotel, downtown St. Louis's finest. I ripened over a long winter in Massachusetts as Betty, shut away from mass meetings and college dances, played wife to her Harvard student in an apartment on the estate of some Boston cousins. She puzzled over recipe books and Dr. Spock's new manual about babies. She peeled an onion down to nothing, then fled in tears to the cousins' cook to ask when to stop peeling. In April 1947 she traveled back to 25 Briarcliffe to have me, and I was born with all the accoutrements appropriate to my station, including a German baby-nurse in a gray-and-white uniform, a Miss Bessie Arnall, assumed to be more scientific about the handling of babies than the Negro servants in the house.

At birth I had a little thatch of black hair, but that fell out and thin, silky blond hair began to grow in. I already sported miniature Conant features: a tiny, turned-up nose and a "generous" mouth. I looked, in short, like a small blank slate of patrician quality. I went off to Harvard at three months old, while my father finished his degree. Because I was a girl, no one thought of me as a life that had replaced a death, the death of dogged, big-spirited Judd Conant. I was more like a roadblock in my parents' lives. The war's urgency had kept them blank slates too; they were just starting to emerge as the people they might have been. I took from my mother nursing and world government, as well as the giddy doings of debutante parties. As for my father, whatever he had wanted to be up there in his Corsair F4U over Okinawa, wearing his flight suit with a half-raw filet mignon from the officers' club stuck in the belt—now he had to come down to earth, to St. Louis, that is, and support me in the style to which my grandparents assumed I would become accustomed.

As if to seal the bargain, I was named Elizabeth, the third in a line of mothers and daughters. There was even an earlier Elizabeth, though not in the straight flush: Biff's southern aunt, nick-named Junie because she was "bawn in June," now living alone downtown in the Park Plaza. None of them used the whole name, though, because that would have seemed too starchy for the homey aura affected by our part of St. Louis's upper crust. So I got a canine tag at birth too—Buff, borrowed from a Vassar chum. Junie, Biff, Betty, Buff.

THE BISHOP HIMSELF christened me one September morning with a small cross of water on the forehead, in the Episcopal cathedral in downtown St. Louis. To the side of the altar backed by its thirty-five-foot-high curtain of stone Gothic saints from 1911, our party stood in the gloom: my two grandmothers in small round hats and white gloves; my father in his white bucks (he'd gotten time off from his new trainee's job at the First National Bank); my mother in a new suit and pumps; my three godparents—two aunts and an uncle who was really a cousin— holding their red Episcopal prayer books. I was a doll-like form in a white lawn christening dress, passed back and forth among the godparents.

In the evening, the inner circle of family gathered at the country club to celebrate with an early dinner. Normally babies didn't appear at the club, but my young aunts had volunteered to take turns carrying me and, if I fell asleep, to sit with my basket in the ladies' lounge, which was really a huge living room for ladies with a bathroom off it, all done up in aged chintz with glass-topped dressing tables. The rest of the party, consisting of grandparents and Aunt Junie, sat in the late-summer twilight, in the humid Missouri air, on the lawn in front of the bar, in gray wood Adirondack chairs with arms wide enough to set down one's bourbon and ice.

My grandparents surveyed the polo match below, listened to the shouts of the children still swimming in the pool behind the hedge, and thought of their dead child. Aunt Junie mourned her dead child too—Sikes Tucker, also a soldier, but one who had died of influenza in World War I. While my grandmother Biff had by now replaced her mourning dress with restrained prints, Aunt Junie was always clothed in shiny black satin, with multiple pearl strands lying on the wrinkled skin of her décolleté. She dressed her white-yellow hair in a Gay Nineties poufed-out bun. In her ears hung the heavy pearls that had stretched her earlobes almost to her jawline. In her speech could be heard the dulcet tones of the Old South. "Your Aunt Junie's gonna be mighty proud of you one day," she said, bending down to the bundle of blankets that was me. After the death of her Alabama husband, the illustrious Mr. Joseph St. George Tucker, which had followed hard upon her son's, she had moved up to St. Louis to join the sister who had married the Yankee Mr. Bemis. That sister, paralyzed by a stroke, had lain immobile and mute in bed for twelve years, while Aunt Junie set her cap for her stern brother-in-law. Junie had lost that bid for remarriage many years before, but she'd stayed on, and there she was still, alone of her generation, a fixture at family functions.

For my grandfather Sam Conant, the host of the party, even with the loss of his son, this was an exultant time. His civic influence was high. Soon he would become the country club's president, and get his picture put up in the men's locker room beside his older cronies'. A few months after that, his next-to-oldest daughter, Helen, would be crowned Queen of Love and Beauty at the Veiled Prophet Ball, the annual society fete (a role that would have been my mother's had she not married). Here he sat now on the evening of my christening, a balding man in a linen suit, presiding over his family of women—his melancholy wife and her irrepressible southern aunt, his younger daughters, all pretty, his oldest daughter with her new and, in his opinion, too-handsome husband (who had had the effrontery to come back alive from the war that had killed his son), and me, the newest member. I was a girl, but I was the first grandchild. My birth was the piece in the puzzle that would ensure the pattern, or so he thought. I was the timeless future.

Yet, looking back, it is not my grandfather but Aunt Junie who seems the most striking figure in my christening tableau. This minor, embarrassing relative was the marker for the fluctuations, the anxiety, the greed, envy, and blocked communication that plagued the family from within. She was an unwitting evil fairy at what was supposed to be an idyllic christening.

Aunt Junie's small capital was supplemented by my grandfather, a fact she didn't know or didn't choose to know, though she wore his gift of a fur stole even in summer. His intervention guaranteed her a place in this world of great lawns, spreading trees, and velvet putting greens, which had remained unchanged through two world wars—as it was supposed to guarantee me a place too. But even if she ignored the fragility of her own position, Aunt Junie must have sensed the fragility of mine. As the family rose to approach the buffet, she volunteered the one remark to my polite young father that seemed to her to represent an all-purpose shield against the evil eye. "Your Aunt Junie's gonna leave you a considerable sum of money," she told him, in a small orgy of vain well-wishing.

M<small>Y</small> PARENTS AND I HAD RETURNED HOME TO ST. Louis from Harvard looking like a family; now the city's social machinery set out to make sure of it. The *Post-Dispatch* ran a spread on "Young Mothers of St. Louis"—square photos of mothers and children scattered about the page, with an oval of my mother in the center, holding me, a dazed one-year-old in a starched white dress and bare feet. At the First National Bank, they doubled my father's salary because, as they said, "We know about that wonderful gal you have at home, and that little girl." On our first vacation at Ludington, a St. Louis watering hole on Lake Michigan, guests looked fondly at Betty in her shorts and shirt, and at bare-chested Henry, digging holes in the sand for their platinum-haired baby to disappear into. "Everybody here adores Buffy—all the little girls play with her," wrote my mother in a postcard to her younger sisters.

Back in St. Louis my grandfather Conant had had enough of our rented duplexes and gardener's cottages; he put a down payment on a two-story redbrick house with black shutters, across a county road from one of the entrances to his own stately subdivision of Briarcliffe, at the head of a straight street of ten houses called Wickersham Lane. We moved into 9 Wickersham in November 1948. As if on cue, my mother got pregnant with a playmate for me. An only child didn't make a real family.

Something was brewing inside my father as well. The banking world he had chosen, or which had chosen him as one of its young soldier protégés, was, in those days, still a world of old men. When Henry and another young trainee, wearing their new three-piece suits, called on a paint-store owner, the old guy asked, "What've they got you kiddies doing?" Days of heeding the hushed mood of money, of following the polished shoes of elders down long corridors, produced in my father a telltale restlessness and daydreams of something quite different from banking: farming. Over the agonized nights that followed the long banking days, he decided to become a farmer—not just any farmer, but a new-style farmer on the frontier of agriculture. He had sprung, after all, from two garden club luminaries, as his parents were known in their set (for the "divine" irises of 35 Briarcliffe), though to date there were no actual farmers in the garden club. My father was painfully susceptible to the utopian aura propagated by the postwar culture. In the pages of *Life,* families in overalls glowed in the foreground of vast furrowed fields; on the nation's movie screens, farmers and ranchers surveyed endless vistas.

There was also a real farming movement afoot, which spoke through the magazines my father read. It urged abandonment of the patchwork fields and row crops that had caused the Oklahoma

Dust Bowl, in favor of long fields following the contours of the land and crops suggested by the nature of the soil. Its prophet was Louis Bromfield, gentleman farmer, patriot, and author, who, from his model Malabar Farm in central Ohio, played pied piper to a generation of returning GIs. Bromfield's 1947 book *Malabar Farm,* which my father carried around like a bible, started with a preamble addressed to a homesick soldier on Okinawa and went on to describe, in diary form, the revitalization of a worn-out family farm he'd bought in Ohio: the seeding of the fields with alfalfa, broom, and ladino clover; the plowing under of those grasses to enrich the soil; the wresting of record bushels of wheat per acre from the soil; the catching of fish in the ponds and the sighting of birds in the trees of his emerald-green "grass factory."

Henry wrote to Bromfield in a burst of excitement, and Bromfield responded cordially. In the spring of 1949, my father took a week's leave from the bank and went off alone to Malabar Farm. He rode a tractor around the curves of the Ohio hills; he talked and joked with the Master late into the night. Then he came back to the bank. At the end of that summer Judson Bemis Conant Kendall arrived, a pudgy baby with a shy, dopey smile, unaware that he bore the entire name of his maternal uncle on the frail back of his father's surname, or that he posed a threat to his father's secret plans. There was rejoicing, especially from the Conants, whose fallen hero was thus officially commemorated. Baby Juddy was settled in the "sewing room" upstairs, across the hall from the master bedroom and next to the nursery where I was ensconced amid white furniture. To doting grandparents, everything seemed rosy and predictable. But a month later, in September 1949, my father abruptly quit his job at the bank. He'd been talking through the nights to my mother, who had agreed to try to escape the tight little world they'd grown up in. With her approval he enrolled in agricultural school at the University of Missouri, two hours southwest of St. Louis in Columbia. He would commute. It was the first phase of a new life.

During the week my mother, the baby, and I were left alone in our new house. For a few months there was a "live-in girl" in the downstairs bedroom, but she was dismissed when a pair of my mother's stockings appeared in her dresser drawer, and a dark suspicion dawned that she'd hit the baby when he cried—a suspicion that came from my own babbling report. So, in a pioneering break from the older generation's nurses and governesses, my mother set out to raise little Juddy by herself, with help from me. We fed him, changed him, played with him, and talked to him. This must have been the start of my mother's special way of looking at me. "Is this okay?" she asked mutely. "Are we doing all right? Are we having fun?" In her glance mingled a puzzled hopefulness about the future, a delighted pride in me, along with a touch of shame about her dependence on such a small person, which implied a mute plea for secrecy.

Around this point I began to navigate back and forth between the matter-of-fact world, in which I was an ordinary child, and the secret world I shared with my mother, in which I was as big and important as she was—in which I was another mother, almost her twin, even her husband, during the week. It was a game to her, but I was learning my role: the precocious daughter, the companion. Looking back, I have the impression that she consulted me about everything we did out of unacknowledged loneliness and compulsive good manners. She'd been taught to show respect for every other human being, including her own toddler-daughter. I responded with as much grown-up spirit as I could muster. "C'mon, Buffer, let's go take the baby for a walk, OK?" she would say, glancing at three-year-old me in that anxious, eager way she kept all her life. "Take a walk," I would echo seriously, and we would dress the baby in his little jacket and go out to stroll around the lane.

This was the time, too, when my mother started sitting down at the piano while baby Judd was sleeping, to play the blues. I don't know why she made jazz her private genre—maybe it was her way of reaching beyond the cloistered emotions she'd grown up in. Her own mother played Brahms and Chopin by the hour, not Negro music. Betty had been uncannily good at classical piano when she was a child, but she had learned new music at Vassar. Her favorite piano pieces became "Basin Street Blues," "Josephine," "Nola," and her own virtuoso arrangement of "St. Louis Blues," which accentuated the composer W. C. Handy's habanera rhythms under the middle section ("Pulls that man 'round by her apron strings") and wound up with a boogie-woogie finish ("Got the St. Louis blues just as blue as I can be . . ."). When she played, there was a charged aura around her, within which great intensity, even passion, could be felt. I have a dim, prememory sensation of curling up at the corner of the couch to hear the music. Or if it was evening and I had been put to bed, I crept from my room and sat cross-legged above the stairs, holding the banister rails. I don't know if my mother was aware of me there, but I became suffused with her: this was the moment I appointed myself her silent listener, the sharer of her every mood, the tuning fork to her internal vibrations.

On weekends my father rudely burst back into the house and into our lives with his news. He already knew more than those old professors at the agricultural college—and anyway, the professors themselves didn't believe that farming could be taught. "Lectures don't do no good nohow," one of them always said as he began his class, and another still favored mules over tractors for plowing. So the dreams of utopia jumped out ahead of the careful plans. Henry quit the agricultural college. He pored over a map of America. He called Bromfield for advice. He was scheming to have a Malabar Farm of his own and, the way his brain worked, he saw things as if they already existed. In this case they almost did: he had found a big piece of unused land he was sure nobody else wanted—government land in Alabama, three thousand acres of the Redstone Arsenal, an old, now-obsolete center of rocket research. Hell, it was prime farmland; why not farm it? Even the government agreed. They gave my father a lease on the Redstone land for ten years, at a dollar a year. He went down to Huntsville, Alabama, and signed the papers.

I can remember nothing of the plan to start a farm; I was too little. But his thinking, reconstructed years later, had a grandiose kind of logic. He intended to grow grass, even more grass than Malabar Farm. And it would be cheap, because it would be seeded from the new, inexpensive Kentucky-31 fescue seed. There would be enough grass to feed three thousand cows, one cow per acre. Each cow would produce, each year, a calf, and the year-old calves would be sold for beef. It would be profitable, and that would compensate, in the psychic dimension, for the money his own father had lost in 1930, when his parents had sailed to Europe to celebrate their narrow escape from the crash of 1929, and no less a personage than Edsel Ford, sitting next to them in a deck chair, had convinced them that now was the time to buy stocks—now, when the market was down . . .

A big farm would wipe that taint of humiliation from my father's childhood, when his family had slid from a fine house downtown to an apartment—a large apartment, it's true, with living and dining rooms, several bedrooms, and a maid's room. Later they recovered to buy the house in the suburban subdivision Briarcliffe. But my father always remembered that day in the early Depression when his father broke down and sobbed because it looked like his company would close. Henry was eight then. Now, with grown-up ambitions honed to a fine point by such half-remembered tribulations, he wanted land, a lot of it. "Just think, Betty," he told my willing mother, who was as prone as he to ab-stractions clothed in images, "we could get away from here. We could stand on our own porch in a sea of grass . . ."

All he had to do was raise the start-up money for the cows and bulls, and for that, his best hope was his father-in-law. Surely Sam Conant wanted to see his son-in-law triumph on his own and his daughter happy. But Henry didn't yet understand my grand-father's controlling impulse where his daughters were concerned and his daughters' children, and how little impact his sons-in-law were to make on his view of the family. There was a decisive scene on the screened porch of 25 Briarcliffe. It was a summer evening, with light from the garden filtering through the screens (the Co-nant garden had blue and white flowers laid out around a dark lit-tle pool). Sam, in his bow tie, sat back enigmatically on the wicker couch. Henry paced the rattan rug. Betty, with me leaning against her and my brother in her arms, looked anxiously from father to husband. About the farming, Sam couldn't say. About the Rocket Arsenal, well, he didn't think it was such a good idea for his grandchildren to go down there. "Henry," he said, removing his pipe, "you'd better settle down and find another job here, where we can be around to give you a hand."

THAT MUST HAVE been the moment when the air went out of my young parents' hopes and out of this new enterprise, their family. The farm project didn't last much longer than that scene on the porch. It wasn't only my maternal grandfather's refusal to help raise capital that killed it, it was my father's failure to project himself outside of the older generation's imagination. "If you boil it all down, it was just one big dream," he said, remembering, years later. "And I didn't have the gumption to get up and go do it at all costs. Anyway, a hundred thousand dollars was big money in those days; it was hard to imagine people being able to raise that kind of money."

My father gave up, at least temporarily, and let himself be taken over by those considerable forces that were pulling him back toward the conventional social scene, a place he could never be happy. My mother, who had subsumed her idealistic impulses in his, sank back into the round of luncheons, children's birthday parties, club memberships, and command appearances at the grandparents' that belonged to the world they'd come home to. It was as if my parents had set out in a lifeboat only to tire of rowing; they had to be towed back and refastened to the bigger ship they'd tried to leave. How did they redefine their marriage, their very selves, as the familiar landmarks closed in about them? How did they look at each other in the night, from one twin bed to the other?

When I was small and staring out of the windows of our house, the first, primal direction wasn't out front toward our lane, but sideways, across the big road toward the entrance to Briarcliffe. That was the way to the grandparents' houses, and grandparents were fixtures of my childhood. They telephoned daily; they scripted Christmas, Easter, and Thanksgiving at their homes or the country club; they furnished the presents that Santa Claus couldn't manage; they offered payments for unaffordable parts of our education; and, from my earliest years, they dropped by. On weekends they strolled down Briarcliffe's winding gravel lane to our house, swinging their English walking sticks.

If it was the Conants, the door would be pushed open gently and we would hear "Where are my precious lambs?" That was Biff—Nonny to us—with her fond and sleepy smile. Sam—Granddaddy—drifted in behind her, beaming proprietorially above his bow tie. If it was the Kendalls, the door would open more forcefully to reveal tall Rebecca—Granny—in her polo coat with the mother-of-pearl buttons, her gray hair marcelled in tiny waves. "How do, children," she would call, meaning my parents too. Plumpish Arthur—Gramp—with his bristly mustache and his child-directed nonsense, brought up the rear. The grandfathers were vague presences; it was the grandmothers who counted for me, as sources of a maternal stability my mother couldn't quite offer, though they were different from each other. Nonny was soft, lavishing us with Christian endearments: we were her little lambs or her angels. Granny was hard; she demanded to be looked in the eye and given a proper greeting, or else she'd make some remark about carelessly raised children.

The grandparents' houses matched the grandmothers. The Conants' old redbrick and stucco Tudor house, where we went almost daily, was cozy and rumpled inside and, in hindsight, a little melancholy. We didn't go in at the front door. We used the back door: up some cement steps—beside which, in the grass, was the mysterious iron lid to a garbage hole, which embodied for me the settledness of the place—into the kitchen, with its old cream-colored cabinets and the buttery smells that swirled around Maggie, the Negro cook. "Is anybody home?" we would shout, and she would answer, "Nobody but us chickens." Then my mother would call out a greeting like a song, as we went through the pantry and across the dark hall into the long living room, where our grandmother would rise from one of the two grand pianos to croon a welcome. Judd and I were allowed to play on those pianos with our small fingers. And we could explore: up the front stairs to visit my young aunts, if they weren't away at boarding school; into the guest room to play with a dollhouse; down the back stairs, where my mother and her brother had once lurked to put toothpaste inside all the Oreo cookies.

Visiting the Kendalls' flat-roofed neo-Georgian house, down the hill from the Conants', we used the front door, like guests. The brick walk to that door smelled like well-bred moss; the gold knocker made a loud knock; the black-and-white squares of the entrance hall gleamed as Granny's pumps clicked ominously across them; the grown-ups' highballs shone amber in the living room. And we didn't roam; we sat still on hard satin couches, swishing the cherries in our Shirley Temple cocktails as grown-up talk swirled above our heads.

Within the same social class, inside the same luxury subdivision, my two parents had been raised with nearly opposite ideas of what was right and proper. The Kendalls were proud materialists; the Conants were as unostentatious and spiritual as they were able to be, given who they were. I can see now, though, that my early sensations about my grandparents were filtered through my mother's. To her the Conant house was homey, the Kendall house alien. After the farm project died, she began to absorb the differences between her and my father, between what he cared about and what she did. Most blatantly, she discovered that my father was not always kind. He couldn't always modulate his temper to the people around him. This realization shocked her. So her Kendall in-laws came to represent some deep core of indifference she sensed in him that coexisted with his charm and his physical magnetism. Her own parents became the symbols of the warmth she was missing. Holding my mother's hands, Judd and I felt her relief when we went up those old back steps to her parents' house, and her wariness entering the Kendalls'. For Kendall visits she coached us beforehand about our manners; she gave us earnest explanations about how Granny was a more formal person than our other grandmother, and had to be treated with care.

Still, the two sets of grandparents shared a public sphere in which we, the grandchildren, counted as valuable commodities—more valuable, it seemed, than our parents. Both grandmothers borrowed us to show off to their friends at charity teas. We were dressed for these occasions in a matching cotton dress and short-pants suit of buttercup yellow or forest green, embroidered with cherries or cross-stitched with our names. "How do you do," we were taught to say to grown-ups, with a curtsy or bow and a frank look in the eyes. Grandparents broke off their golf games if my mother drove us past the golf course, and came over to the road to talk to us. They took us to lunch on Saturdays—or rather, my grandmother Conant did—at the Women's Exchange. She picked us up in the bone-colored Cadillac whose radio was always playing opera from New York, and drove us downtown to "Ladies' Mile," where the ornamental facades of

Saks and Montaldo's smiled richly across the street at the cement-colored art deco storefront of the Women's Exchange.

The quality whir of the Cadillac motor and the fine tones of the car radio, piping in that faraway sound of culture—such sensations acted as balm on my small, anxious psyche. It was easier to be a granddaughter than a daughter, and more rewarding. Part of the Women's Exchange was a shop with rows of dresses and boys' suits such as I and my brother were wearing (made by poor women to be sold by rich ones—that was the "exchange"). It was, for me, the epicenter of "good taste," which proved my own worth. Through the shop, under an archway, you came to the tea-room—and that was like the stage.

Oh, the clatter of plates on glass tables, and the ubiquitous drawl of grandmothers! There were grandmothers everywhere, with their heavy gold bracelets and cigarettes and graying hair arranged in tight curls. They were greeting the guests behind a tall desk. They were working the cash register. They were sitting together at all of the tables in their tweed suits, with the furs draped on chairs, some of them with small polished children squirming opposite them. And they were glancing, both directly and circumspectly, at me. "Here are my precious grandchildren," Nonny always announced to her friends Midge or Tollie or Etta as she ushered us ahead of her through the door. The friends would then smile at my bright dress and red shoes, at the matching little brother I held by the hand. "And *doesn't* she have that wide Conant mouth, Biff, and your round cheeks!" they said.

Sometimes unexpectedly, the person greeting the guests would be my other grandmother, Granny, tall and acerbic, with her cigarette smell. Then a different chorus of friends—my two grandmothers were friends themselves, though coolly—would chime in to remark on the "something fine-boned in her forehead that looks just like you, Becky." I didn't have to do anything; I just stood there as whispers of identity drifted across my person.

It was a strange, asymmetrical sandwich of grandmothers. The one behind me, with her eyes that crinkled at the corners, was the one I belonged to. But it was the one in front of me, the supposedly alien one, who fascinated me. I would stare up at the crisp pleats on her nylon blouse or the pucker of lipstick on her cigarette holder as she leaned down to give me an ironic greeting. She had been a businesswoman during the Depression. Impelled by the family's waning fortunes, she had gone to work at the home-decorating department of Scruggs, Vandevoort and Barney, where she had risen rapidly to the post of director, only to return to genteel idleness when the war brought prosperity. What she displayed in her person, though, was what eluded the Conant side of the family: a worldly authority that was feminine. And I, as my mother's protector, was looking for that.

IT WAS BECAUSE of my father. At home, his personality dominated our family, at least on the surface. I can see him in memory, moving about the yard on those Saturdays when we got home from the Women's Exchange. My mother received us, removed our starched cottons, dressed us in corduroy overalls, and sent us outdoors to be near him, like actors who'd switched plays. As imperious as his mother, my father strode about in his khakis and a tight white T-shirt, laying new lawn turf, putting out the sprinklers, digging tree-sized holes on the edges of the property, hauling young holly trees with their roots in burlap bags to fill the holes, ripping up the brick terrace, carting sand and bricks for the new terrace in his wheelbarrow, disappearing into the garage to feed his chickens, releasing his pig from its pen by the garage, tending his pair of Canadian geese who waddled over the grass.

After the farming plan had failed and there was no job, Henry, at age twenty-nine, went to work at the new firm of Longstreet Abbott, which pioneered in "commodity counseling"—farm-related work, though not outside with grass and dirt and cows. Longstreet Abbott advised the big feed and grain companies of America, starting with its parent company, Ralston Purina, on what crops to buy, so as not to be caught out with a surplus or deficit. He offered to work "for free, sir, till I can learn the business." But he'd been hired for pay, even without an Ag-Econ degree. The bosses liked his drawling deference, his family connections, and the fact that he'd kept his pilot's license current. He would fly them to meetings in the company plane. My father also turned out to be good at buying and selling imaginary quantities of soy and alfalfa and pork bellies. On weekends, though, or on summer evenings—any time he could be outdoors—he dabbled in real farming, while my brother and I played nearby.

The job with Longstreet Abbot allowed my father to save face, since it wasn't the bank, and commodity trading held possibilities for the quick riches that he dreamed of. But he must have known, deep down, that he'd settled for a diminished existence. That's why all his work on the yard had a manic quality. Home became the place where my father could "let off steam," or escape into his all-consuming projects. Even in my earliest years, I remember a potentially explosive quality in him. Sometimes he laughed and picked up my brother or me and roughhoused with us. Often he ignored us, unless we happened to cross his line of vision. "Hey, little fellas, take off your shirts and get some sun on you," he'd say if he saw us playing in the grass. I obediently became a small bear cub tumbling in the sun with my brother cub, feeling the sun on my shoulders. I raised the garden hose from the grass and took a bite of the cellophane arc of water, like he did. Such actions stood in for the relationship with my father that I didn't know I lacked.

To my mother the picture looked like a family. According to the unconscious bargain my parents had struck, my father was allowed to be stormy and self-absorbed; she remained earnestly interested in everything he did. She had us participate too. She took us out to gather the eggs from the chickens; she reached our hands through the bars of the pig's cage to tentatively pat the animal, whose name was Peewee. She tried very hard to play at this farming. A snapshot from 1952 shows her kneeling in front of a white picket fence in jeans and a white shirt, holding a large white chicken. On either side of her my brother and I stand in overalls and straw hats, looking expectant. On my mother's face is a puzzled and hopeful smile.

In the definitive first skirmish of my parents' marriage, my mother had won. She hadn't meant to win—she'd been genuinely excited about the Alabama farming project. In the end, though, here were my parents, still in town, with two small children to keep them there. My father was tamed. My mother didn't quite know what to do with her victory. She was too busy trying to please everybody, playing the young society wife outside the home and the adventurous mate for my father within it. We led quite a schizophrenic existence. We were the smart young family of the upper crust; we were the wholesome young family of the heartland. We wore the handmade clothes of the well-bred; we wore the store-bought clothes of the fifties masses. We moved back and forth daily from one mode to the other, changing from overalls to dress-up clothes, dress-up clothes to overalls.

Underneath the surface another family hovered, the invisible, unnoticed, and almost unremembered family of the three of us at home—my mother, brother, and me. That family took up most of daily life, a life that was filled with characters from books, like golden-haired Little Lord Fauntleroy or black-haired Mowgli, or lusty songs that my mother sight-read at the piano from the *Fireside Book of American Folk Songs*. In that secret family we had long conversations about why things were the way they were—everything from why a father got mad too often to why a soap bar got smaller when it fell in the water. My mother had backed into a marriage that meant more loneliness than she had bargained for. Her emotional food came from the daily improvisation of raising us, when she could become a girl again and reinvent her mother's wistful coziness.

I was the key to the equation, the steady little presence that made my mother feel better. Even at the tender age of four, my inner self was defined by her puzzlement, her longing, her deferred visions of the wider world. And what a thrill it was, standing up in the bathtub at night behind my little brother as he sat and splashed, to feel the importance of my small soapy person— to feel that I was somehow embodying the brave new worlds my mother had once dreamed of for herself.

THE BRAVEST OF THE BRAVE NEW WORLDS FOR MY mother, or rather, the key to all the brave new worlds, had been college, because of her own mother's deferred ambitions. My grandmother Biff Bemis had longed to go to college in 1918. She had been serious and bookish, like the father she adored. But that father, Judson Bemis, forbade it. He said college was for girls who wore masculine shoes. He himself had married a southern belle, Martha, the sister of Aunt Junie. Instead of college, he sent my grandmother, at eighteen, with her female cousins, on a white-parasol tour of the Bemis jute mills in India, where she contracted typhoid fever and stayed on alone in an Indian hospital with only her religion for solace. It was when she came home from India that she met my Princeton bon vivant grandfather at church, and married him at twenty.

So, through that spark of unrequited longing that can jump from mother to daughter, my mother was raised by *her* mother to be a College Woman, which meant, in my grandmother's stubborn and melancholy mind, something like a lady preacher. The transformation can be seen in Betty's childhood photo albums: the blond baby sprite on the beach, laughing in a nineteen-twenties jersey bathing suit, gives way to the serious five-year-old in a nineteen-thirties party dress and a bow at the side of her hair, sitting cross-legged on a rug and eyeing the camera with the pure resolve of a little soldier. Judd, the bigger brother, with his cap of blond hair, sprawls amiably next to her in the picture. It seems he got their mother's uncertain and eager heart. Betty, all unknowing, got the impulse for revenge.

Biff Bemis Conant makes only a few rare appearances in her daughter Betty's baby album. In one photo she's an awkward figure in a cloche hat, posing in bright sun in a driveway; in another she sits indoors at the piano, a slim, dark-haired woman absorbed in her playing; in another she's caught earnestly talking in front of the stone wall of the Episcopal cathedral where she spent her time volunteering. You sense Biff's desire to shrink from public view, while her daughter, in adjacent snapshots, grows up eerily focused on the world. Betty at eleven, with braids, between two trees, receives the camera's gaze with a curious poise. Betty at thirteen, with curls, on the screened porch, looks up from her book with that same pure stare. In group photos you can pick out her intent chiseled face from rows of disheveled teammates holding hockey sticks, rows of blousy campers in white shirts and middy ties under a spreading tree, or—older and closer up—a row of student council members seated sternly at a long table, anchored at the end by Betty, their president, in a tailored gray jacket and a hairdo with bangs.

Then Vassar, the promised land, where my mother joined the revelries and the cancan lines of coeds improvised for snapshots with a shy confusion. Frivolity was endemic to college life, but try as she might, her socks never slouched, her shirt never untucked. To the other girls she was sweet and serious and, to a few, so picture-perfect as to seem unreal—"the naivest person I've ever met," said one when I asked her on the phone about those Vassar days. That naïveté made my mother a magnet for the shining ideals and the jumble of New Deal convictions and Wendell Wilkie visions that Vassar in wartime held out to its young women. "I'm on the hospitality committee of the Church Conference on 'One World,' " she wrote her mother excitedly in her first month, "have to have dinner tonight with a colored educator *and* with the *President* of the *College!*" "Psychology, History, Comparative Religion, Debate," sang the parade of postcards picturing ivy-covered college halls. In the first dizzying year my mother spent at college, 1944–45, the world was opening up—a chance to work for Peace, for the Brotherhood of Nations, for the Betterment of Mankind . . .

My mother didn't plan to leave college at the end of her second year. Something between the shock of sexual attraction and the vision of being a selfless life-companion to my intensely insistent father took over her mind. Marriage happened, then children. She'd wanted children. But somewhere along the way she must have looked up and understood that she'd gone off course. The exalted existence Vassar once held out had contracted, almost by itself, to the well-lit domestic circle her mother had occupied.

. . .

IN THE SUMMER of 1952, when I was five and my brother two, my mother found a way to go back to Vassar and to take us with her. The school had a four-week summer program, the Institute of Family and Community Living, which taught married Vassarites (and some graduates of other colleges) the scientific approach to the lives they were leading. It also took their children off their hands, even those as little as we. We were to be housed separately and cared for, kibbutz-style, twenty-four hours a day, while our mothers concentrated on their studies.

The benefit of this arrangement to the mothers was obvious; to the children, less so. Segregation of parents and children was an unthinking holdover from the earliest years of the summer institute. In 1926, when it was founded as the Institute of Euthenics, a turn-of-the-century metaphysics of domestic well-being, American child-care specialists still lingered in the nineteenth century, thinking of children as miniature adults who needed discipline more than affection. Dormitory living was supposed to teach them the one and wean them from the other. In the thirties and forties, psychoanalysts fleeing Europe had brought news of childhood's vulnerability, but the separation of children at Vassar persisted. By the fifties the communal children's school at the institute was being justified by a different model: Anna Freud's wartime London nurseries, in which teachers, small peers, and "daily stabilizing rituals" stood in for the parents misplaced in the London blitz. Or so said the institute's brochure. In 1952 on the peaceful Vassar campus, our mothers were to stop by once a day after breakfast to check on us; on Sunday afternoons they could take us off for two and a half hours of familial play. Otherwise, we were to be small guinea pigs set loose in a world of "rich and bal-anced" stimulation, coaxed, observed, and monitored by a battery of child-care experts and their student apprentices.

I had been forewarned of this separation—I would be helping my mom go to school, she said, and when we got back home in the fall, *I* would go to real school too: kindergarten. Still, it was a shock when we arrived at the old, tree-shaded Vassar campus to be installed in a liver-colored dormitory with high gables along with the other four- and five-year-olds, to see my mother waving good-bye from the front door. My little brother wasn't even with me; he'd been put with the babies in another building far from mine.

My reaction was severe. Where once I had swooped around my mother like a magic bird, swelling and shrinking to her sig-nals, improving her moods with remarks that did their best to paraphrase hers, now I was just another child, plodding along in a line on nature walks. A tentative, lonely outrage informs these memories, which are unusually sharp. They are the first memo-ries of myself alone, without my mother, and they are centered around my longing for her that surfaced when she got within range. I can remember one of those Sunday reunions, when my mother and I and my little brother, reunited, played a game on a rug, and the sweetness of home came back to me. Afterward, standing at my high dormitory window, I watched my mother leaving me again, riding away on her bicycle, a small figure get-ting smaller as she rounded a circle of crimson flowers and ped-aled out of sight.

Otherwise, that time at Vassar blurs into dullness. I was too young to separate impressions of places from my sense of myself. The bright-lit dormitory corridors and the bare walls of my dor-

mitory room: these bleak pictures seemed to merge with my
physical being. I, too, was bleak and unadorned. No kind teacher
made an impression on that isolation; I remember only a little boy
in my dorm who wore red sneakers, whose sturdiness reassured
me. In the evenings on the dorm's front steps, I sat next to him
and planted my feet wide apart like his, trying to turn into the big
girl my mother daily told me I was. She didn't notice my depression—she had trained me to match my need of her to her capac-
ity to respond. She herself was too young and unsure to doubt the
child-care experts, who emphasized the stimulation that Judd and
I were getting away from her. Not even those experts caught a
glimpse of the numbness in the recesses of my well-groomed little self. "Friendly," "industrious," "an example to the other children," said the reports they gave my mother at summer's end,
noting only that I "sometimes needed encourgement to rely on
my own resources instead of turning to my teachers for valida-
tion."

MY MOTHER, MEANWHILE, off in the Gothic splendor of
Blodgett Hall, was filling up pages and pages of a brown spiral
notebook with the neat pencil-printing that was her handwriting.
How to divide up a household budget, how to get spots out of different fabrics, how to choose clothing to flatter a complexion according to the Munsell system of color notation, how to organize
one's neighbors into committees to get things done, how to bring
up well-adjusted children and teach them religion—a jumble of
topics big and small, the glassy-eyed mixture found in Vassar's euthenics. Euthenics had been dreamed up in the 1910s by Ellen
Swallow Richards, a Vassar graduate turned sanitation engineer.

Bedridden for a time by the chronic rejections of male colleagues, Richards rose from depression to apply her scientific approach to the woman's domain and invent a new field of expertise that eventually became home economics. And Blodgett Hall, financed by Richards's wealthy disciple Minnie Blodgett, became its center.

The Euthenics Institute's founding mission had been to rectify the woeful ignorance among college girls—upper-class girls—about matters of housekeeping, a condition that had prevailed far beyond the 1920s. Cleaning, washing, and cooking were not things my mother had practiced, growing up in the thirties in a houseful of servants. Even in wartime she had sent her laundry home from Vassar to St. Louis every week, where the laundresses and seamstresses attached to 25 Briarcliffe washed, pressed, and mended, then sent it back.

Now she was learning those practical skills she'd been improvising through six years of marriage. In later years she would mention this or that housekeeping trick she'd picked up at Vassar, or cite the Munsell color wheel when we bought clothes. But by the early fifties, housekeeping and good grooming were not the institute's main focus. The real excitement lay in the esoteric secrets of child care, imparted in the summer's biggest lecture course, the only one required of all the student mothers, Family and Child Development.

It was taught by a fifty-three-year-old psychologist, Mary Fisher Langmuir, director of the institute, whose daily lectures addressed mothers with an uneasy mixture of cheer and suspicion. According to my mother's careful notes from that course, mothers shouldn't try to mold children; children molded themselves, passing through the growth stages articulated by Erik

Erikson (Oral-Sensory, Muscular-Anal, Locomotor-Genital, and on up the line). Mothers should be referees, or discreet social scientists, studying family members and mediating among them. This approach had a political dimension. In line with other progressive institutions during the early Cold War years, Vassar held that a "mild regime" at home created self-knowing little democrats, while an overstrict one bred mindless fascists or communists (by now judged to be the same thing). The success of this democratic task depended not just on what a mother did with her children, but on who she was with her husband.

Marriage, explained Mary Langmuir in my mother's notes, allowed a woman to practice "love and companionship" with another person; to learn about "one's own sexual needs and one's 'mate's' "; and to make, with that mate, a "Great Affirmation" (i.e., a baby). If hypocrisy or frustration crept in, Langmuir warned, the whole family—the whole nation—was in danger. "Biggest challenge, to work out our own relationships so as to leave children free to lead own lives," my mother wrote down carefully, along with, "This generation has trouble with sex, because girls think of using their minds." Not even thrice-married Mary Langmuir, with her upswept curly hair and her cheerful manner, could banish from her course that bogeywoman of fifties pop psychology, the unfulfilled wife whose sexual frustration fastens, vampirelike, on her children. My mother was already terrified at not being sexual enough. The memory of her body comes back to me, attractive, slim, but never aglow with the sensuality that signals sexual satisfaction. I think she was consumed with worry about whether she was woman enough for my father. I can almost feel it through the faintness of her pencil jottings from that faraway summer of 1952. A plaintive note in the notebook's margins says: "Adolescent Character and Personality—check into this, for *me*," as if she didn't quite believe she'd made the transition from girl to wife.

If Mary Langmuir's child development course fanned my mother's deepest fears, another child-related seminar that summer, Religious Education for Pre-Schoolers, offered her the comfort she would draw on for the rest of her life. Its teacher, the lean and leathery Reverend J. Howard Howson, had been her favorite Vassar professor in her undergraduate years. He had opened her eyes to the world beyond Main Street, sending her out to a synagogue and a Catholic church for comparative purposes.

Perhaps Howson was the real reason we'd come back to the Institute. By 1952 he'd changed with the times and narrowed his focus, like Mary Langmuir, from the world to the family, embracing Langmuir's gospel of intrafamilial tolerance. But Howson emphasized the religious part of the picture, which rescued my literal-minded mother from the terrors of self-inquisition, at least for the moment. Thanks to her own mother's lifelong retreat into religion, Betty could embrace any crusade labeled Christian. Howson's course removed conjugal harmony from Langmuir's guilt-ridden domain and put it back with Christian duty. Besides that, the rituals Howson proposed for spiritualizing children—bedtime prayers, grace at meals, holidays, and churchgoing—were the old-fashioned ones my mother knew from her childhood. To fit them to a new progressive time, all she had to do was make them child-friendly.

VASSAR PERFORMED A smoke-and-mirrors trick on my mother, changing her humble role in life to a grand one, giving her a secular religion in which a questionable marriage was wrapped up in the bright public sphere of expanded motherhood. Upon our return my mother wasted no time in putting this newfound purpose to use. That fall of 1952, when she was twenty-six, she took over the education department of our Episcopal church, St. Peter's. St. Peter's was a new redbrick Georgian Revival, reposing on a bed of tasteful gray gravel at a green crossroads close to our house. Its white walls, clear windows, and red cushioned pews suited my mother's native optimism, just as the mock-Gothic cathedral downtown, with its dark wooden pews and its stained glass, suited my grandmother's melancholy. The moment was ripe for Sunday school curricula. Episcopalians in those years were catching up to Presbyterians in the incorporation of child psychology; the famous Seabury textbooks were in preparation.

My mother plunged into a melee of curriculum experiments, which she kept track of at home by means of index cards in shoe-boxes. At church on Sundays she became a personage. When we streamed into the church from the parking lot, people would grab her elbow to tell her something urgent, or she would reach over people to touch a shoulder and remind the person of something. Before the sermon, when all the children processed downstairs for Sunday school, my mother processed too, tall among us, shepherding us to our classrooms.

At home, too, after Vassar, we had all kinds of ceremonies. My little brother and I said prayers in our room before bed, kneeling on prie-dieux, low chairs with sad purple pansies embroidered on the seats by my grandmother Conant. We said grace before meals, folding our hands and bowing our heads over our plates. Other rituals emerged in our household that were only distantly connected to God, such as making gingerbread men at Christmas, so that we would learn about giving as well as receiving as Vassar had promised; or skipping and galloping to my mother's piano-playing, so we would grow up to love sonatas and symphonies. Strictness was not the point; even in church we could read our own storybooks or color in our coloring books. We were supposed to be finding our own way to belief. But when I think of myself as even a partial participant in my mother's religion, I get a feeling of detachment. She believed in God and in worship; I was always a skeptic.

When she sang out the hymn, her face upraised, glasses flooded with light, her clear voice serving as a beacon to the timid and befuddled voices around us, I felt embarrassed for her. When she began to intone one of the communal prayers that started at the back of the church and engulfed us in its tide ("I believe in one God, the Father Almighty, Maker of Heaven and Earth . . ."), I thought she spoke too loud. She was putting herself on display. Everyone could see what she felt. On the other hand, I knew I lacked my mother's goodness of spirit. In prayers at home I wasn't the pure and contrite little being she wanted; I watched my own small figure from above to check on my angle of kneeling. I couldn't lose myself in what I was saying: I had to pitch my voice to the particular ring of spontaneity that I thought would please my mother, childish greed tempered with generosity of spirit. "Please God, bring me a stuffed horse—and by the way, take care of my grandparents, my aunts, my mother and father, my teachers, etc. . . ." Perhaps it was my forced separation from my mother at Vassar that had planted this seed of detachment in my hitherto obedient mind. I wasn't what she wanted me to be.

Except when it came to the most charged and solemn moment of the new family religion: my father's daily return from work. There memory puts me in tune with my mother's beating heart. A hush came over the house. The casserole was baking in the oven, the dining room table had been set by the two of us. I can see us, my slim mother in a fresh blouse and wide red belt, bending over the table to make sure it looked right; and five-year-old me, my soft blond hair combed in a neat pageboy like hers, straightening a knife or a fork. My three-year-old brother played on the living room rug, but not too messily. Toys had been cleared away. Across the forest-green expanse of rug, the front door seemed to pulsate with suspense. What would be my father's mood?

On good days he came in excited, the cold still caught in his hat and coat, announcing, "Betty, we're rich," or "Wheat did OK," or "Soybeans selling well." Such a cheerful salvo meant he would join us, sort of, in the dinner conversation, reading aloud from a news magazine propped against his drink, peering at us to ask, "Did you ma-linger today?"—we hadn't, he just liked the word—drawling lyrics of songs like "Your cool and limpid green eyes," or repeating old jokes: "I opened the window and influenza, heh heh heh . . ." On bad days, he slammed the door as he came in and shouted, "Turn on the exhaust fan for Chrissake Betty we're living like pigs!" Then we were in for a grim dinner, with some mutterings about "margin call" and "weather crazy in the corn belt," from which he escaped early into the night, out to the chickens and geese and the pig, who kept him better company than we did.

The fact is, my father was the eternal dissenter, the cannibal to my mother's missionary. He spoiled things with his compulsive irony. I don't think he set out to make a mockery of my mother's careful family ceremonies; it just happened. He fidgeted in church—it looked spontaneous but we knew it wasn't—and smirked when he walked by during our prayers. It's true that he worked in a profession that rearranged his hopes and fears daily. But the real culprit was a perverse streak in his very personality that made him allergic to the anxious piety drifting toward him from my mother's direction. Or else it was his ever-simmering rebellion at just being in a family.

At the dinner table his nonsense mixed with mockery incited my mother to giggles, or reduced her to tears. Perhaps in their first years of marriage his mood had held sway over hers; now Vassar had fortified her. They were an even match. The contest went on night after night, sometimes lighthearted, sometimes bitter, causing scenes and quivering voices, causing a collision of naughty mirth with pained forgiveness. We two children sat low, turning our anxious eyes from one end of the table to the other. Down there was my mother, so pretty, leaning forward, her eyes beseeching behind her glasses. Up there was my father leaning back in his button-down shirt and bow tie from work, with something bright and irresponsible emanating from his person.

I was famous for getting indigestion in the middle of dinner and leaving the table to "rest" on the living room couch. My brother often sat out dinner alone. He was a delicate child, with myopic dark eyes and long, curling eyelashes that required special eyeglass frames—and he was a near genius, or so they said at Vassar. In her lecture course Mary Langmuir had played a tape of his two-year-old voice lisping through a vocabulary prodigious for his growth stage. But he showed the strain in his own way. He fell silent at those family dinners and could be found afterward in his room, maneuvering his plastic cowboys and Indians and "buckling bronkelings" in endless skirmishes, intoning a fantastical commentary. He also had bursts of gaiety when my father wasn't there. We three flew down to Key West in February 1953 minus my father, who was to join us later—one of those abrupt vacations furnished by the commodity market. Juddy made up a song while strapped to the airplane toilet seat that my mother fetched me to the bathroom to hear: "The people down below the clouds think it's a cloudy day," he sang over the droning of the big engines. "But we know where the su-un is, it's up above the clouds!"

I felt proud that at three my brother could already picture the abstraction of the world below the clouds. But I was only five myself—well, almost six—and I occupied a strange position in the family: I was a child, yet also a parent to my brother. He and I sometimes giggled uncontrollably together or locked each other in wrestling holds. These moments didn't affect my basic picture of myself; I was not part of his generation, but part of my mother's. "Pretty and earnest, just like Betty," said my father about me, and he'd chuckle dismissively.

I deeply felt my mother's need of me, though she never talked about it. I wasn't just her acolyte in the family religion and a stand-in parent who made sure that my brother got the praise our father failed to offer. I also served, during some suddenly empty midafternoons, as a receptacle for the memories of Vassar in its giddy wartime days. I was treated to lessons in zigzagging over the floor to a Charleston hummed under my mother's breath, toes-touching then heels-touching. I was taught risqué songs she'd once learned on dates, such as "Passengers will please refrain / From flushing toilets on the train / While standing in the station / I love you. . . ." Even as my mother inducted me into the ranks of future wives and mothers, she also consigned her premarriage world to me, that buried world of college flings.

I received womanly confidences too, such as the revelation my mother handed me in Key West just before my father arrived. Outside, noon glared through the open windows of our rented bungalow. "I want to tell you something that may be hard for you to understand," she said as she sat me down on the wicker couch. She told me that her stomach would soon start to grow big, and in a few months, I would have a new brother or sister. "The man and the woman get close together," she continued, "like they're hugging, and something that looks like a tadpole jumps over from him into her, and a baby starts to grow from it . . ." This sounded very odd. The rest of the talk included the information that if you didn't want to have a baby right then, you put something like a teacup inside yourself. Perhaps she added the birth control details because she wanted me to have the full picture, her own mother having told her nothing at all. With or without a teacup, this thing that the man and woman did resulted, she said, in "the most wonderful feeling in the world." That was the confusing part. I believed her about the mechanics of babies; it was part of a mysterious store of information that would someday be useful. But I was puzzled about the "most wonderful feeling"—or rather, I was jealous.

For all my allegiance to my mother, I was quite drawn to my father at that time. The Key West trip coexists in my memory with a burst of longing for him—or else a longing for the ocean. I had fallen in love with the Florida ocean outside our bungalow door, the shimmering expanse of it, its magnifying ripples when I stood in its shallows, its softness at shell-colored twilight, its sudden agitations in a storm. In my father's absence, I had conceived the idea that he was the person to understand this passion. His bursts of manic energy, his fits of impersonal tenderness, even his stalkings off in the night at home, seemed to match what the ocean did. I looked forward to his coming, still hopeful that he would recognize me as a kindred spirit.

But my eager overtures were rebuffed. He showed up abruptly, a day before he was supposed to come. I was off playing in another bungalow with a little girl from Virginia. I heard the commotion of his arrival and came tearing through the white sand between the bungalows to find him—a laughing, shining, teasing father. After he joined us, though, I see myself in memory as a lackluster little figure on the beach, with the haircut of a clown—my hair had just been cropped to midear—and a speech pattern I couldn't get rid of. I said "Yikes!" all the time. "Yikes, look at that wave"; "Yikes, there's a jellyfish"—crude little word-flags sent up in case my father was looking my way.

Still, my father's compulsive naughtiness had begun to have an effect on me. I was looking for experiences that took me out of my mother's virtuous part of the world and edged me toward the rougher seas of his sensations. It was a strange dilemma. In everyone's eyes I had signed myself over to her. I was her helper, her table-setter, her confidante, her twin. I had her ear. I didn't have his. As a result, I swallowed my father without his participation, and he lived somewhere inside me, creating a small cold place within my generally virtuous glow, a hard germ of naughtiness and of calculation. Sometimes I found myself yelling at my mother the way he did in an attack of temper. "I hate you. You pick on me." Once, when I did that, I was sent to sit alone on the living room couch "until I felt some better feelings." Murderously sullen, I waited and waited, then I sprang up and went to her in the kitchen. "You won't believe what happened," I told her with wide-eyed guile. "God came to me and made me feel peaceful. I think it was a miracle." Her grateful smile terrified me.

I was also secretly drawn to two pictures my father had hung on the wall of the stairs opposite the front door, sketches of falcons done in deft strokes of charcoal on brown packing paper in black frames. I used to stop on my way through the house and stare at them. One showed a hooded falcon in profile, sitting on a jeweled leather glove at the end of an arm, backed by a castle with a turret and a peaked roof. The other showed an unhooded falcon sitting on a wooden fence, looking back over its shoulder toward the same castle while the hood dangled from the fence. The pictures, I learned later, were drawn by Otto Kals, Germany's master falconer from before the war. My father had learned about Kals from a 1940 book on falconry. After the war he didn't think about where Kals might have been (though a group of Nazis headed by Goebbels had practiced falconry); he just worried about his prewar hero. Sometime in 1946 he wrote on an impulse to Kals, Düsseldorf, Germany—and he heard back. He sent some relief packages of dried milk, tobacco, and anything else Herr Kals ordered in his imperious and spidery script. Kals's thank-you pictures had come in the mail, and now they hung in a position of honor in our suburban house.

It's striking how far apart my two parents were from each other, my mother with her religion of family, my father with his emblems of escape. They'd each kept adolescent dreams alive, with the depths and motives hidden from each other. I boomeranged between them, trying out my father's adventurous longing while still angling for my mother's approval. On Easter Sunday of 1953, when the children of my Sunday school were hunting Easter eggs on the grounds of the girls' school across from our church, I took a rest on the porch of the school's kinder-garten cottage. A Sunday school classmate, pudgy Louise Gardiner, was lounging there too, with her raven-haired older sister, Mary Lee. I was interested in older girls, to whom I could show off. Appraising Mary Lee, I remarked politely that I knew all the numbers. She appraised me back and told me there was one number I didn't know. What could it be? My complacency fled. She said it was Zero, no-number, nothing; less than all the others. My, what a concept. Zero glowed with a bright depravity. Basking in the glow, we conspired for me to spend Easter night at the Gardiners'. My mother agreed, though I could see the hurt in her eyes. She was very pregnant, and I would miss dinner at the grandparents'.

That older girl, black-haired like my father, master of his ni-hilism, in cartoon form: how could I resist an alliance with her? But I couldn't sustain a life without my mother, not even for one night. At twilight we three little girls, utterly spent from hand-stands and cartwheels, repaired inside to the Gardiners' lamplit living room, where a card table had been set up for us with a white tablecloth and a plate of toasted cream-cheese sandwiches. I surveyed the scene, which included old Oriental rugs, small-paned windows, and a balding Mr. Gardiner across the room in an armchair, reading a newspaper (a sorry picture of a father, I thought). I took a bite of a sandwich.

The taste turned ashen. A roaring started in my ears. Some leaves, lit a poisonous green, brushed the window from out-side—was there a storm coming? Pure terror set in. Mrs. Gardiner's concerned face became a bruised fruit, and Mr. Gardiner shrank to monkey size across the room. Amid the roaring all I could hear was "Mom, Mom!" and it was my own voice. "Mrs. Gardiner," I focused desperately on her face, "please, please call my mother, I have to go home."

My mother was consulted by phone. She spoke to me in the calm tone reserved for our special talks. She told me I was her brave girl. The Gardiners hovered about. I agreed to stay the night. But at that undistinguished moment I lost my bid for independence and spontaneity. I consigned myself to a long stint of bewildered virtue, the price of keeping my mother at my side.

Chapter 4

I T WAS THE FLOOD OF BABIES THAT TURNED ME INTO A
lost soul. In the years between little-girlhood and middle-
girlhood, one is supposed to start choosing one's own friends and
trying out in their company all the big human issues of loyalty, be-
trayal, camaraderie, integrity. Instead of venturing outside the
family to do this, I was pulled in the other direction: back toward
home.

My mother produced not just one but three babies between
1953 and 1957. If there existed time-lapse photographs of our
house from the mid-fifties, they would show it beginning to shake
and tremble—as if beset inside by a pack of circus clowns—then
overflowing into the surrounding landscape. The screened porch
on the front corner swelled to a glass-enclosed protuberance, a
new "family room." The garage next to the house begat an identical white garage beyond itself, the first garage having metamor-

phosed into two new bedrooms. The asphalt of the driveway crept over to meet the new garage doors. The backyard reached out to embrace the adjacent vacant lot—which my father bought—creating an unbroken expanse of Technicolor green on which sprouted jungle gyms, log cabins, sandboxes, and in 1958 the suburban coup de grâce, a shaggy palomino pony who looked forlornly over the fence toward the county road.

I don't know why my mother wanted to transform her compact pair of children into an ungainly brood of five. Perhaps repeated pregnancies reassured her of the viability of her marriage. Perhaps mothering little babies satisfied some hunger for physical affection that gnawed deep within her, a physical need that was, probably, the explanation for her own mother's five children. Or maybe Vassar had just convinced her that producing Great Affirmations in the form of children was a noble goal for educated women. At any rate, she plowed forward in the fertility enterprise, to which my father contributed his sperm, his salary, his small windfalls from the commodity market (the losses went unrecorded), and an attitude of laissez-faire bemusement occasionally tinged with cruelty. In hindsight it seems he had little to do with how the family was shaping up, outside of the plans to alter the house and expand the property. My father had a passive streak in his nature; maybe he just reacted, instead of thinking ahead. He was also away a lot, flying his company's small plane around the West, making presentations to brewers and flour millers.

Besides, the zeitgeist supported large families. In the affluent and sleepy Eisenhower years, things like new babies seemed to happen without consequences—though in our house, the actual births were far from stress-free. In addition to the suspense of the packed suitcase waiting under my mother's bed, the abrupt departures for the hospital in the middle of the night, the returns home when she stepped out of the car smiling tiredly at a new bundle, there were continual near catastrophes. Boy baby of 1953—Henry Jr., or Harry—came early, and was "awfully little and scrawny" (my mother's notes in his baby book) at five pounds. Girl baby of 1954—Margaret, or Mardy—threatened to eject herself even sooner and was secured by means of the "miracle" fertility drug DES, but even so emerged at four pounds. She was so tiny, red, and wizened that she had to live in an aquarium in the hospital (that's how it looked), with my mother distractedly commuting back and forth. Girl baby of 1957—Faith—while still in the womb, a fetus of three months, was violently jolted when my mother tripped on a rusty swing at a nursery school, then poisoned by a tetanus shot to which my mother reacted with an elephantine swelling of the joints, requiring massive doses of cortisone. Faith was born apparently unscathed in August, but my mother almost died a few days later from another freak accident caused by exercising too soon in her hospital room. She got an embolism in her bloodstream that stopped just short of her brain. Rushed to intensive care, she came back from what she later described as the luminous corridor of death and, after six weeks, brought home a strangely sleepy baby.

In and among these crises, all of us grew, and my mother became a larger-than-life figure in her circle of friends. Having started a family earlier than other women her age, she was blazing a trail for them; she had become a living guidebook to what would happen as their families increased. The other young mothers could look at us—always well-groomed and alert, if numerous—and see that it could be done, and happily. My mother was good at handling us, almost too good: it was a kind of performance. At the club pool she could watch a toddler bob in the water, coo at a baby, listen to an older kid's question, signal to the swim coach, and hold a conversation with a friend in the next lounge chair all at once. At church she managed to get the flock of us from the car to the pew and keep us all quiet during the service.

Nor was my mother's maternal persona just for public consumption; she displayed her ambidexterity at home too, like a proud athlete. In one arm would be a baby, in the other a notebook, a pencil, the telephone. When you spoke to her, she would look up brightly from something else, as from an inexhaustible but slightly surprised fount of attention. Under her selfless exterior my mother harbored, I think, a small thrill of vanity about the figure she cut as she trailed through the country club amid symbols of her own fertility, as she strode into my school's granite halls laden with babies. In a 1954 photo from the society pages of the *Post-Dispatch,* she is modeling a cuddle seat (an early version of a sling seat) for the Junior League country fair. She looks pertly off into the distance, wearing a tweed jacket, a string of pearls at her neck—and baby Harry slung on her chest.

Ever alert to my mother's subtle signals, I turned serious about the mothering profession. Now it wasn't a game, as when I'd mothered little Juddy; a helper like me was needed in our baby-care factory, though we'd acquired by then a live-in Negro maid (we said Negro in those days), Maidie McCurry. More to the point, with my mother always busy, proving myself dependable became the route to her affection. After Harry's birth in 1953, I learned how to carry babies and feed them their bottles. I protected the soft tops of their heads and supported their necks. I was good with diapers: I received the dirty ones from her, dunked them in the toilet, put them in the hamper, and basked in my mother's proud smile of thanks. In public, too, at church or the club, I played second mother, hefting the littlest baby or shaking a rattle to catch its attention. I displayed animated interest in the babies of my mother's friends. Those young mothers were my friends too, since I didn't fit in with their children. I was older and bigger, a generation unto myself. They watched me, I could feel, with something like longing. "I'll be happy if little Susie or Kathy grows up to be like you, Buffy," the garrulous ones confided.

Some internal static followed, though, from my enlistment in the mothering ranks. When I was six, just after Harry was born, I withdrew to the powder room every night after dinner and threw up. Dr. Martz, our bow-tied pediatrician, was consulted; he asked my mother how much time she was spending with me. The result was an institution called "Time," which made me feel a miser and a squanderer. On nights when she could manage it, my mother came for a half hour to my new room next to my brother's, remodeled out of the former garage. That half hour was all mine. We could talk, read, listen to folk songs on my small record player—whatever I wanted. I could never tell when she would come; I waited under the covers with the lamp on, as if for a lover. She would slip in the door almost soundlessly. "Mom, hi," I would say, and stretch luxuriously, even though I knew that, as I kept her captive, the baby's demands were piling up outside my door.

The doctor's orders seemed to work. More time with my mother made the vomiting stop; I came out of that troubled phase at seven, or so it seemed, and took my place as her definitive "big girl." The Christmas card of 1954 proudly proclaims it. Families like ours sent Christmas photographs of their children posed prettily in armchairs by a fireplace. My mother posed us in 1954 as the Holy Family, against the most desertlike wallpaper in the house, the subtle stripes of the dining room. I am sitting in the center in veil and robe, looking up with a shy smile. In my arms is a tiny baby in a trailing blanket—my new sister, Mardy. On one side of me stands my dazed five-year-old brother Judd, also in a robe, with a towel tied on his head—he was Joseph. On the other side a toddler looks excitedly out at the camera, one-year-old Harry in a white nightgown, with wings strapped on his back— an angel. Here was early proof of my mother's flair for homemade propaganda: a Disneyesque picture of Christian Americana.

THE PROBLEM OF losing my childhood to the babies wasn't as easily remedied as my mother thought. It was 1954 when Judd and I moved downstairs to the two shiny, white bedrooms that had been made out of the old garage. My mother was proud we each had a room and a brand-new bathroom for both of us. But we were lonely down there. We were far from the upstairs center of the house where we had been; we were out beyond the kitchen and the back door. My mother could hardly hear if we called in the night. It was as if we'd been banished to the outer regions, or discarded downstairs, while a new young family usurped our for- mer upstairs room. I can barely remember now what those new rooms looked like, except for a sensation of flimsiness. Once, in a fit of temper, I slammed the new bathroom door against the wall, and the doorknob burst right through, leaving a jagged hole. An- other time Judd and I had a violent disagreement; I pulled all the drawers out of his new dresser and spilled the clothes on the floor. The dresser almost toppled over on me; it must have been cheap.

My mother couldn't focus on our discontent, but Maidie, our resident nursemaid-housekeeper, did. Her room, next to the kitchen on the first floor, was midway between the two parts of the house. If I called for my mother in the night, Maidie came out wearing a white dressing gown, her oiled hair down on her shoulders—a woman, suddenly, out of her uniform. It was she who relayed the call upstairs by calling "Miz Kendall, Miz Kendall." In fact, Maidie's image offers the only route back to the frustration that lay unacknowledged beneath the supposedly contented family surface—and to my own long-buried misery.

She came to us in the spring of 1953, just before Harry was born. St. Louis then had an ever-expanding pool of domestics because of the country blacks from down south who kept filling up the ghetto, a section of old brick houses north of the main downtown and close to the river. Our city was a key stopping place on the migration route of Negroes up from the rural South. "Halfway to heaven" was how one black civic leader explained it: where blacks ran out of money or courage or both. Maidie McCurry, late of Winona, Mississippi, found us through a newspaper ad my parents placed for a domestic. I opened the door myself when the doorbell rang. There stood a coffee-colored woman in a worn navy-blue coat, clutching the newspaper. She had oiled hair pulled back in a bun, gypsy earrings, a broad Indian nose, little pince-nez glasses, and a prominent bosom. She was in her mid-fifties. She and my mother sat down at the dining room table and talked. My mother offered tea. There was some confusion about her name. Not knowing that "Maidie" was an old Scottish name, I was amazed that her parents had foreseen her future occupation at her birth. The next day she moved into our extra downstairs room at the back of the stairwell, bringing her hair unctions, black bobby pins, threadbare dresser-doilies, and armchair anti-macassars.

The conventions of the times were cruel: she lived in that cramped bedroom in the midst of a noisy family. She earned, I think, forty dollars a week, working nonstop in her starched gray uniform with the white collar and white apron, returning to her other invisible life downtown only on Wednesday evenings, Saturday nights, and Sundays. In this pre–civil rights time, she was supposed to be dank or bad-smelling or even somehow old-fashioned. She said "er-um" as she was speaking, and she chewed something brownish like wet tobacco. That suggestion of alien bodily juices explained, in my mind, why she had to wear a starched and pressed uniform when she came out of her room. That room was strange and dark when I looked through the door-way. I longed to go in; perhaps I could become another kind of daughter in there. But we weren't allowed in Maidie's room. "It's her private place," said my mother. On those Wednesday after-noons and Saturday evenings, a low-slung, rusty car came to pick her up and take her to an even more private place somewhere in the recesses of downtown. Yet this supposed human fault line be-tween her and us, this problem of an inferior yet menacing aura of "Negro-ness," was bridged whenever we kept her company in the kitchen or sat against her in the family room at night, watch-ing TV when my parents were out.

In some way Maidie saved us all from emotional starvation. It was as if a real adult had moved into our house—and my parents knew it. My mother paid Maidie the compliment of uncon-sciously speaking like her. "Miz Kendall, I'm fixin' to go upstairs to make that bed," Maidie would say. "You come on up, Maidie, I'm fixin' to come down with the baby," my mother would answer. Maidie must have reminded my mother of home, not just of the servants' voices from her childhood, but the voice of her mother, which slipped so easily into southern-slurred fondness. Maidie made my mother calmer, tenderer—and my father more polite. He used to take his BB gun out in the yard and shoot squirrels for Maidie—she liked squirrel stew—which he presented to her with a courtly flourish. And, of course, she soothed babies and toddlers with hugs and smiles and soft singing.

But I, the big sister of the household, came in for her special attention. I went to school at Ladue Elementary School down the road. (My mother believed in public schools—they were part of the Vassar civic legacy.) Always a favorite of teachers, I wasn't doing so well among my peers. I'd been my mother's equal in my own mind too long to know how to talk to girls my age. Maidie quietly offered herself as a sounding board. One day as she made my bed in my former garage room, I laid out the girl politics of the second grade. I described blond, slouching Janie Hanser on the playing field at recess, the most "popular girl"; and curly-haired Kristy Kircher, who did everything Janie said. I confessed to my unfavored status in the outer rings of their devotees: "I look all right, but I don't know how to make the jokes they make." I can remember the view through my window out onto the driveway as I gave myself up to the pleasure of conjuring away hurt through ever more voluble descriptions of playground events. "How strange that saying all this to my *maid*," I thought, "should make me feel better."

Nor was it just a one-way relationship. Maidie saw me as a near adult, a possible friend for herself, or so I imagined. Sometimes she would give a great sigh in my presence and tell me she was tired. Or she would look off in the distance and quietly sing

"Swing Low, Sweet Chariot," while I stayed very still. One day she beckoned me to the dining room window that looked out on our neighbor's yard. "You see that man?" she asked, pointing at the neighbor's "hired man," who was raking leaves. "I married his father yesterday." I was thrilled to be trusted with this grown-up information and stammered out my congratulations, though I was terrified that being married meant she would go away.

The status I thought I had in her eyes gave me the freedom to let her see my own guilty secret without my having to explain it. I had become obsessed with food, especially with desserts or anything sweet. This condition seemed to be the reverse of the earlier state that had caused me to throw up every night. Maidie, in charge of breakfast, had taken to making biscuits from scratch, which we ate southern-style with butter and syrup. But she only made them some mornings, if the spirit moved her—or if I looked sad in the evening. Then she'd whisper her biscuit-making plans for the morning, and I would brighten. Here was something for me alone. When I woke up, I would smell the sour-dusty smell of the biscuits in the dark and feel myself near tears.

My obsession with food puzzled me. It seemed to have invaded my mind against my will. I found myself thinking all the time about what there would be for me to eat and counting up the minutes until I could eat it. I was trying to fill myself up and bury a misery I couldn't recognize. But the suggestion of a greedy soul living inside me terrified me. I feared I was worthless. The feeling grew acute in the summers in New Hampshire, when I was eight and nine. In 1953, three years earlier, my Kendall grandfather, Gramp, had bought a white farmhouse with a red barn in the White Mountains, the summer landscape of his boyhood. Visiting those grandparents became a family ritual.

Every summer we drove in our red Volkswagen bus over prairies and mountains to the farm, and the sunny chill of the place called forth everyone's deepest appetites. My father, ever the Robinson Crusoe trapped in a family, took off his shirt and shot bows and arrows, or jogged along the dirt road, scanning the tops of trees for hawks. My mother recovered the robust girlhood spirit of Camp Pinelands, her earlier New Hampshire utopia, and took us tramping up mountains. My scrawny brother Judd, shadowed by little Harry, became a habitué of the deep, dark woods through which he slipped soundlessly on pine-needle turf, like an Indian. Baby Mardy sat in the clear air in my grandmother's garden, blue mountains rearing up all around.

And I made my mother stop the car at the Maple Museum, the Rock Shop, Santa's Village, Clark's Trading Post, in the hopes that she might buy me a special rock, a ring made from a black-smith's nail, a little balsam pillow stamped with a pine branch. They all laughed at me for that, saying I was in love with the gift shops. But food counted even more. In the mornings I slipped into the New Hampshire kitchen to read the menus my grand-mother Kendall wrote out in her forceful hand for the cook. At noon I sat in the living room while the grown-ups drank highballs under a clipper ship in a gold frame, waiting for the moment when the menu would materialize in the dining room. On picnics I grabbed a sandwich before the others, to make sure I had one. My mother got mad at me. "You've always understood about sharing, why are you doing this? Why have you turned so selfish?"

She wasn't only mad, she was worried about how I looked. As my mother was having babies, I was getting fat, not obese but chubby. At seven I was just a little puffy, still cute and girlish. Be-tween eight and nine a roll of extra flesh appeared around my middle. Then I lost my baby teeth, which left gaps in the front of my mouth. All of a sudden I wasn't pretty. I can be seen in family pictures at the sides of the group, smiling distractedly and sitting a little hunched, my long hair pulled back in a headband, my feet crossed in new saddle shoes. By ten, in the fifth grade, I was hefty. I had two long braids and an overeager smile, with the new front incisors slightly crossed. I liked it when my mother brushed my hair and braided it in the morning; it was our ritual. But as she pulled the braids tight, I could feel the color draining from my inner being and the animation leaving my face. It was as if she were pulling my spirit into submission.

I STARTED TAKING ballet in the fourth grade with a group of girls from my school. Once a week a different mother drove us into our suburban town to the ballet school, down some stairs from the Shady Oak movie theater. I was expected to be good at it, because the elderly teacher, Madame Cassan, lived across our lane in a white house with a rose garden. She was really Mrs. Burridge. She had met her husband in some Asian sea, while she was touring with Anna Pavlova. He had been an admiral on a ship. They liked my family, and even just me. I was talkative; I dropped in for glasses of water and cookies on summer days. I got the first yellow rose from their garden in spring. And I loved the fact that proper English Mrs. Burridge had an alter ego at her school, where the vestibule glowed pink from shawls thrown over lamp shades and she wore a tunic and ballet slippers. Photos looked down from the wall of a satin-gowned Pavlova with a mysterious, gap-toothed smile. But in the dressing room, as we littler girls of my carpool peeled off undershirts and climbed into leotards, I encountered the wobbly flesh of my torso. By the time we filed into the airy oval studio to stand at the ballet barre, I had been neutralized by self-loathing. I could feel Madame's disappointment from the front of the room as I woodenly repeated the exercises.

My mother started to talk to me about cutting down on bread or taking a smaller piece of cake. For ballet class she sewed me a short wraparound skirt to tie over my leotard and make me feel prettier. It was reversible, so it was really two skirts—a print fabric on one side and turquoise on the other. I remember her holding it up at the sewing machine: "Won't this make it more fun?" But my mother couldn't help me much, since she was struggling then with her own femininity. Something was draining away from her—the dewy atmosphere of privilege and beauty that had accompanied her since youth, the assumption of her shiningness—or she was banishing it herself. She cut her hair short in late 1953, for convenience's sake. She waved it with an arrangement of bobby pins at night. She switched to darker lipstick, which in the photos of the family album looks almost black. She changed to cat's-eye glasses frames, but they combined strangely with her native earnestness. In the family portraits she looks neat and collected but also tight and distracted. She was always smiling in photos, that upbeat smile that meant "we are such a nice family." In 1955 and 1956 my mother was still in her late twenties, but she was making a decided switch from debutante to schoolmarm.

And she was compelled, unconsciously, to take me with her. In the fourth grade, the same year I started ballet, I grew obsessed with the story of Cinderella. The Junior League put it on as a play in our school auditorium. I was moved to tears by the heroine's grief as she leaned on her broom in a crystalline light; I was raised to rapture when the fairy godmother appeared from the wings and dressed Cinderella in lavender. With a hint of my old boldness, I conceived the idea that I could act out Cinderella's rescue and ascension. Girl twins from Sunday school lived in a big stucco house on the other side of the country club. I went to play there sometimes, in a raised octagonal room off their living room that suggested a stage. My mother, who was between babies, agreed to organize some of my regular playmates and their mothers into a theater group. But she decided to use the occasion to mix public school families with Sunday school (country club) families— at the time, a daring social experiment.

We had one of our little talks. "You know," she said gently, "you have a higher social position than most of those other girls. Wouldn't it look snobbish if you played Cinderella?" In despair I ceded Cinderella to Janie Hanser, who didn't need the lead role, since she was still the tyrant of our playground. Janie had her blond hair curled for the occasion. I played the ugly stepmother, wearing a faded, green grosgrain gown of Aunt Junie's stuffed with a pillow, my hair poufed up in a frightful bun, and two red circles lipsticked onto my cheeks.

My mother, deep inside herself, was excising feminine frivolity in favor of civic responsibility. She thought the two were mutually exclusive. But in the process she was blocking me off from my own dawning femininity. What was worse, when my young aunts came home, my mother looked dowdier and I chubbier. My mother's sisters, blond Gigi and dark-haired Jane, were coming and going at this time from boarding school and college. At the country club, in their off-the-shoulder blouses and cinch belts, they wandered with their dates down to the edges of the pool at twilight while we children were still laughing and shouting in the water. If I rode my bike up to 25 Briarcliffe, my aunts allowed me to stand shyly in the corners of their rooms while they dressed for dates. Sometimes I answered the door to the young man: "Hi, she's upstairs, I'm the niece." My aunts bestowed on me old charm bracelets, discarded rhinestone elephants that said IKE in the middle, lipsticks in scuffed gold cases. They led me down the hall to view their pearl-encrusted gowns lying across beds in spare rooms.

In 1957 my eighteen-year-old aunt Jane made her debut parading serenely on a white cloth across the cavernous Kiel Auditorium to a sort of altar, where she was crowned a Special Maid of the Veiled Prophet Ball. It was a civic ceremony dating from the city's Gilded Age, when secret fraternal rites were routinely clothed in Central Asian garb. I was there in a box, a pudgy ten-year-old with white ribbons in her braids, looking down on a future of fragrant femininity. But I was already half-resigned to the idea that such a future was not for me. My mother sat behind me, pale from the latest baby's arrival and her near-fatal accident in the hospital room. She was worrying, I knew, about that baby's condition at home. One minute I leaned out over the great auditorium, my imagination flying out to my regal young aunt as she gave her deep curtsy; the next minute I sat back guiltily to be nearer my mother. Back and forth I bobbed in my confusion of allegiances. Deep down, though, I wasn't mother or debutante, just some jolly court jester, stuck between duty and desire.

MY FATHER, removed from the world of babies and children I shared with my mother, still hovered darkly over the whole family picture. As my mother and I drifted away from womanliness, he approached some vigorous core of manliness. He was a big man already. Now he got heftier and acquired a fifties crew cut. His face looked rugged; his body seemed to jump out of his clothes. In snapshots he almost always wore a tight white T-shirt, like an athlete or a worker. He was still masterful around the house and yard, fixing faucets or closet doors, putting up fences outside. He began lifting weights every night in the basement and went on weekend camping trips with business partners. My mother dutifully pasted the photos from those trips into the family album: a page of children playing in the backyard; a page of my father sitting in the back of a canoe with laughing men; my father holding up a fish he'd caught by some Ozark lake.

In the context of our family, my father's physical vitality carried a misogynist edge. He became less patient wih my mother's table-manner lessons, her child-level talks to us on kindness. "Betty, you should have married a minister," he would say as we sat down at the dinner table, giving his infernal chuckle. Sometimes it was a relief to laugh with him, and after a pause, my mother would laugh too. But besides his casual mockery of her, he became unsettled by the way *I* looked. I could feel his fastidious distaste whenever I came near him, since he didn't bother to conceal it. He took to calling me "Big Butt." "Hey, girl," he'd say as I passed him in the yard, "you've got quite a butt on you." He didn't pursue me to persecute me; his remarks just happened when I got within his range.

I'm held in a muffled despair when I look back. By that time I didn't have any hopes left of being the tomboy I'd once half tried to be, though I mourned the loss of my skinny younger body, which had matched my brother's. But I could see that my brothers didn't have it much better. Judd, still undersized at seven and eight, was put to work every weekend hauling trees, picking up sticks, moving piles of bricks. His nickname was "Pinhead," not much kinder than mine. Harry joined Judd when he came of age. With the second son the paternal contempt paled to impersonality and he was "Bud." If my father assumed that a daughter could be scorned with humorous irony, he believed that a son could be co-opted for slave labor. Protest wasn't possible for daughters or sons in the conventions of our family. Nor did my mother confront my father about his treatment of their children. More than anything, she wanted us to be a family—and for that to be true, she needed my father to be a father. To confront him would imply that he wasn't. There was also the extra right he still held in their marriage bargain—to indulge in mockery, to have a fit of temper, to exhibit some weird extra-manliness as compensation for that half-remembered, earlier failure to be a farmer.

The real trump card my father held for me and my siblings, and probably for my mother, was his crazy, intermittent charm. For all his menace, he still represented, in our household, the possibility of surprise, a break from routine, a sudden leap of life that got you out of the doldrums, even at the price of your own shame. Sometimes, too, a kind of throttled affection would leap out from him at one or the other of his children, even at me. Once in a while he came home from work and announced that he was taking me and Judd to the amusement park, Kiddieland, off in the country near the airport. There, inside the gates lined with lightbulbs, on the grass strewn with ride tickets, he became a devilish and indulgent comrade. Such occasions kept a belief alive for me that somewhere in a parallel universe was a ghostly father who loved a ghostly me, as my mother always assured me he did. Once, when I'd burst into tears at losing a black pearl ring that had been my mother's, my father presented me with a new ring, a white pearl with his initials inside the band.

And he bought me a pony. At ten, with sexual feelings stirring in me despite my self-disgust, I fell in love with horses. I'd had horseback-riding lessons earlier at the country club, but this new vision of horses belonged to another realm—to pure fantasy, to Cinderella desires. I longed irrationally to possess a horse that would surge powerfully under me, more powerfully than a bicycle or a pogo stick. I spoke about it all the time. My father, to my astonishment, did something about this. One day in 1957, a mangy little palomino pony showed up at our house in a horse trailer; my father had found it for sale on a farm in the country.

Such isolated fatherly gestures play tricks with the past. I remember almost fondly the years when that shaggy, mean little pony lived in a lean-to in our vacant lot, when I rode it up and down the lane with my legs dangling ludicrously, looking like the foolish youngest son in a Russian fairy tale. But it is my mother's myth of the family that I remember, not my own view of things. The end of the new-baby years did turn hopeful for my father, and therefore for her. In 1958 my father made another bid for professional autonomy. He left his big brokerage firm and joined up with two young commodity brokers. He thought we were going to be rich. Crop prices were rising; American farmers ruled the world. A killing could be made in the market by young and irreverent traders, a hope which made his family bearable again.

On weekends he packed us all into the Volkswagen bus, even my mother and baby Faith, and drove us out to view the crops he speculated on daily. He'd hang halfway out the bus window. "Alfalfa coming along; soybeans look good," he'd say about the rows of green plants striping the rich river-valley earth. My father had a new hobby at home too, connected not with land but with sky. He was making a giant telescope to study the stars, grinding the lens with another lens (that's how you did it, two disks of glass wearing each other down). The Russian sputnik had made everybody star-conscious, and he was going to show us the stars and meteors and satellites. He even brought us into the lens-grinding process. He sat us down every evening in the living room along with the neighbors' kids while he shone a light through the lens to test it.

The neighbors helped sustain this moment of fragile and anxious well-being. Since February 1957, the eccentric and numerous Combses had lived in the white house next to ours. When they moved in, preceded by bicycles, tricycles, jungle gyms, playpens, and a rooster in a cage, we discovered that they matched us in size and age, except for *my* Combs, curly-headed Toni, who was half my size, and their extra baby, Georgie, who crawled around, ate cigarette butts, and had his stomach pumped every few months. They were a benign double of our family, a replica of us without the strain; even the stomach-pumping was treated as routine. They were Catholics, which meant they were supposed to have a lot of children, or so my mother explained to me. Besides that, Edmee Combs stood to inherit the Schaefer beer fortune, a fact my father spoke of in private with naked envy.

What helped most was the Combses' ease with their children, which spilled over onto us. Big Bill Combs, an overgrown cherub in glasses, organized ball games with his boys and my brothers, and he supervised the construction of a six-story tree house. Edmee Combs called each of us—grown-ups and children alike—"Doll" or "Honey" in a raspy voice, endearments I responded to like a thirsty plant. All four parents genuinely liked one another. My father sat outside for hours with Bill Combs, drinking beer and chuckling. They barbecued together, piles of hamburgers for all the kids. The mothers—Betty, tall and golden, Edmee, dark and spicy—made the salads in each other's kitchens. That summer of 1957, they turned out to be pregnant together. They waddled around like Tweedledum and Tweedledee.

But there's a darkness under the memory that isn't just my own misery, suppressed in the family picture. Real catastrophes started to occur at that time. Both those births went wrong. My mother had Faith first, almost dying of the embolism; Edmee Combs joined her in the same hospital, even in the same room, and had a baby with cerebral palsy. Little Dickie Combs came home from the hospital with crossed and stricken eyes and weak limbs, though he seemed happy enough in the frothy brew that was the Combses' life.

One summer evening almost a year after those births stands as an idyll on the edge of darkness. The two fathers are sitting in plastic web chairs on the Combses' driveway by the smoking barbecue, talking of astronomy as pale Venus rises in the twilight and Sputnik circles overhead. In the branches of the oak tree above them, the bigger boys, nine-year-old Judd and eleven-year-old Billy Combs, are hunched in their tree house, shouting down taunts at the littler boys, Jerry Combs and Harry, both five, who lurk in the bushes and stare up with longing. Inside the Combses' lit screened porch the mothers, daughters, and babies are gathered at the table. Edmee is feeding the damaged Dickie, who lolls out of his high chair—he was always having to be propped up. My mother sits beside them holding our baby, Faith, who is shaking a bracelet and squealing strangely. Around the table the two little girls of four, Mardy and Lulu Combs, are circling in fairy-princess

tatters and wielding magic wands as three-year-old Georgie grabs
at them from under the table.

I sit next to my mother at the table, my usual polite and un-
happy self. Toni Combs and I always sat close to the babies, ready
to help feed them or take them from our mothers. Toni seems in
hindsight to be contented with the job—she smiles her elfin smile
as she pats Dickie. Not like me, the ungainly beggar at this family
feast. I can't feel anything about this me—not her anger or her
longing: only her dullness, the tight waistband of her shorts, the
wrongness of her new cropped hair. My mother and I had decided
a short haircut for me might be more grown up.

It was the moment just before my family started to spin out of
control. I was an uneasy marker, a symptom of the wistfulness
and the recklessness waiting there under the surface.

ONE DAY IN AUGUST 1958, MY NEXT-TO-YOUNGEST aunt, blond and clever Gigi, who was twenty-one, was talking to my mother outside on our brick terrace by the big oak tree. My mother held one-year-old Faith in her arms. The sky was darkening toward a thunderstorm, and a sudden high wind rattled the leaves. "Betty," said Gigi, drawing on a cigarette and peering at the impassive baby, "it's weird, Faith doesn't see the leaves. There's nothing in her eyes."

By this time Faith had learned to pull herself up on furniture. She was babbling and making sounds, but the sounds didn't have any sense, not even the beginning of sense. Faith had her own special aura within the family. It came partly from her religious name, also the name of a distant matriarchal Bemis cousin. And my mother seemed to remember the close brush with death she had right after Faith's birth—this baby meant life.

When tiny, Faith had lain quiet in her crib for long periods of time, then squealed for no apparent reason, though she went through prolonged spells of crying too. Unlike most babies, she was not afraid: even strangers could pick her up and bounce her around. But other people besides my aunt had wondered about her reactions. When Faith was six months old, Edmee Combs leaned over her crib for a long time, then asked my mother if she didn't think she was slow. All of us had been slow, said my mother. But the doubts increased as toys were held up to Faith's unresponsive face and shouts were tried on her passivity. "Christ, maybe she's deaf," said my father, one day in late August when he found my mother standing in the back hall with Faith in her arms. He clapped his hands loudly by Faith's ear. She didn't move. He clapped by the other ear. Same thing.

It was as if those hand claps released all the questions my mother had kept quiet so many months, the fears entertained and rejected, the growing conviction that this small being wasn't proceeding through the Vassar growth sequence like her other babies. In the fall of 1958 a battery of tests began on Faith—ear tests, eye tests, reaction tests, measurements of her muscles, her coordination, her nerves, her attention span, her brain. Her hearing tested normal. That was bad—something else was wrong.

The mood of the family tightened as it became clear that Faith's brain was damaged, though no one could say how much. It was a diagnosis that never quite happened, at least not for us other children. My mother wasn't softening the information; it was coming to her in bits and pieces. Nineteen fifty-eight was the tail end of the era that had hidden retarded children away in tiny rooms, shut them up in institutions, removed them from medical knowledge. Retardation, before the Kennedys came to prominence in 1960 and made it a cause, was assumed to be a form of mental illness. In 1958 a diagnosis was still an uncertain proposition, especially in the case of a child like Faith, who didn't look abnormal. Moreover, the syndromes that can accompany retardation—seizures, stunted growth, neurological deterioration—were not then part of diagnostic experience. Faith showed signs of these conditions, but no one factored them into the whole picture. The word "trainable," a bleak term that meant the opposite of "educable," was tried out; the word "autistic" was thrown around.

My parents tried to hide their confusion and grief from us, but even my father was shaken. I thought at first Faith's condition made a kind of sense. I was finally at the age when a baby seemed a perfect companion instead of a secret rival. Faith would be a baby forever, like Dickie Combs—who would want her otherwise? But the gap between her appearance and her behavior grew weirder as she grew older. She was dressed in what we all had worn as toddlers, crisp cottons from the Women's Exchange embroidered with cherries or chickens or bunnies. Her hair, fine and almost blond, hung in a shingle cut. Her eyes were wide and green. She wore white baby shoes, in which she took her first steps.

Her body continued to grow and learn, leaving her mind behind. She started to totter alone. Then she could walk faster. She lurched about and squealed. She went pommeling toward a bracelet someone held out, or snatched the glasses from someone's face and had a fit, squealing and shaking them like a banshee. She couldn't focus on you, but she could feel you, and if you felt familiar she would scream with pleasure. Sometimes she grabbed a part of your flesh in her fist and squeezed. And she could destroy things—dolls with weak limbs, glasses of milk, plates of food.

The furniture was taken out of Faith's room except for the crib and a soft armchair. A wooden gate was installed in the doorway so she could zigzag in that bare room, here, there, picking up a toy, shaking it, dropping it, shuffling after another. She staggered back and forth like a little drunk person. Music helped quiet her. She liked hearing hearty songs ("My Blue Heaven," "Bye Bye Blackbird") sung by the Mitch Miller chorus on a record player just outside her room. My mother could quiet her too and spent hours with her in the armchair in her room, repeating words to her and singing her songs. The doctors thought that with careful stimulation and love, Faith might learn some basic things. They were wrong.

"He's got the whole world in His hands," sang my mother. "Hanss, hanss," echoed Faith. That didn't mean she was learning a word. She had found a sound that intrigued her synapses-less brain, and the sound went into her ear and out her mouth at random. Her brain was an eight ball to which sounds floated from a minute to a week ago. "Ah-ah-ah," she'd say suddenly, the three-note sound meant for placating a rag doll, or "Ah ah dee de da da day oh," which was the beginning of "I've Been Working on the Railroad." My mother kept trying for words. "Baby?" she'd say in that hopeful lilt she used with Faith, holding up the rag doll. "See the baby? Say 'baby?' " "Eee—eee," responded Faith with unholy glee, snatching at the doll and giving way to a sound that wasn't human at all.

Maidie took up the slack as never before, carrying Faith around, handling her with a brisk tenderness. But my mother seemed to think she alone could quicken Faith to normalcy, using endless repetitions or ingenious games. Hence the hours in Faith's room. My mother had resolved not to hide her. Faith went everywhere with us—to the country club, to the grandparents', to parties at other families' homes. My mother found an unexpected ally in my grandmother Biff, the original baby-worshiper, whose religion equated this "blessed lambkin" with the baby Jesus himself. When we visited 25 Briarcliffe, my grandmother took charge of Faith. Elsewhere, Faith was such a handful that we all became nurses, stepping in as needed, picking her up, matching my mother's "Faith voice." "See the birdie? Hey, Faithie, look at the birdie . . ." We also did "Faith duty" outdoors, after school and on weekends. The boys roughhoused with her, rolling on the grass as she crowed with glee. Little Mardy was attached to her on a leash and boinged around the yard at Faith's whim.

I carried Faith on my back up and down the lane while Toni Combs carried Dickie on hers. Dickie still had crossed eyes and a lolling head. He was a picture of woe. Faith, jiggling and grabbing my hair, was a picture of hysteria. We trudged up and down the lane with these weird little beings on our backs, proof that the fifties dream of family had blown a fuse. The feel of their clinging bodies reached down into our muscles and our very selves. Through the subterranean logic by which girls of nine and eleven understood such things, Faith and Dickie became something besides persons; they were pieces of persons, pieces of a family—the pieces that had gone wild and disobedient. So it seemed for all us siblings, and the Combses too. You couldn't look at a group of round-eyed Combses without seeing traces of the woe that was Dickie's; you couldn't look at us Kendalls without glimpsing Faith's manic self, her chronic impulse to take off and zoom right out of life, like a gas balloon.

. . .

AS MOMENTOUS AS all this was to my mother, and therefore to me, it wasn't the only thing in my mind. I was beginning to get a glimmer of who I was outside the family. School and the world of peers were finally weighing in.

I was in the sixth grade. I had floated dutifully through the elementary grades and emerged as "original." So said Miss Glaser, the school's star teacher, whose stern-jawed face shone with a lovely light when Independent Initiative appeared in her pupils. Susan Gillerman and I were her pets, and we outdid each other trying to find oblique approaches to straightforward assignments. Studying serfs in faraway Russia, we made up a serf and gave him a name, a home, and a bunch of ragged children begging at his fence. Susan Gillerman was my best friend, the first friend not sent by circumstance, but found, recognized, in a moment of clarity.

It had happened at school one evening the year before. We were there for the Christmas pageant, uneasy in our party clothes, excited that the familiar halls were lit up. I was washing my hands in the girls' room in front of the mirror. So was Susan, a shy, stick-thin girl with a wild, sharp face framed incongruously by a sleek blond pageboy. I'd been in school with her for six years without paying much attention. "You like music, don't you?" I asked her on a whim. "Uh-huh," she said. "Do you like Tchaikovsky?" I asked. "Too emotional, Beethoven's better," she said, and I nodded with satisfaction. There were such people, it seemed, who slipped into your secret inner dialogue as if they'd been there all along.

Earlier in my childhood, music had been so prevalent in our house as to seem part of the furniture. Over the years my mother had continued to sit down at the piano at odd moments and play her ragtime and blues. I had taken classical piano since I was five, as had my brother, both of us progressing through flights of bumblebees and "Für Elise." In fourth grade I'd added violin; now, in sixth, I was about to approach the instrument seriously, with gruff Mr. Vandenburg of the St. Louis Symphony. I was scared he might find out I'd relied so much on my ear I barely read music. I had a very good ear, I'd discovered at six as I played a game at the piano, hiding my eyes and naming the notes I sounded on the keyboard. When my mother saw what I was doing, she looked almost scared. "You have perfect pitch," she said. "What's that?" I asked. "It's when you know what a note is without reading it from music," came her answer, in which I felt, without comprehending, some awe.

Now, in the sixth grade, the knowledge that I possessed a musical penetration superior to my mother's became important, because the willfulness that had abandoned my character in the chubby years was emerging again. I was still chubby, but so were other people in my grade. I no longer saw myself as a giant among pygmies. Or maybe the diminished self-loathing came from my family's preoccupation with Faith. There wasn't the old pressure to be happy, since something was actually wrong. The crisis over Faith had shifted things; it gave me the space to be imperfect.

So far, my rebellion was musical; it consisted of disowning Tchaikovsky, of whom my mother approved. Meanwhile, Susan Gillerman, the daughter of a mother more determinedly bohemian than mine—a graphic artist though married to a scrap-metal dealer—had fallen in love with opera. St. Louis had a fervent cadre of opera-lovers who mounted amateur productions in the summer. It was chic to be part of them—my two youngest aunts sang in the chorus. Susan Gillerman had latched onto opera naturally, at a young age, and played *Tosca* and Wagner constantly on her record player. Now the sudden friendship that had sprung up between us seemed to confirm to our mothers that we were meant for higher fates. They didn't say this. But when we daughters talked about fame, adventure, and eternal friendship, our mothers' eyes shone as if from distant girlhoods.

My mother, moreover, considered this friendship a social experiment in the making, with a religious dimension. Susan came with us to church, hunched over in the pew with shyness. I went with the Gillermans to synagogue and wasn't shy at all; rather, I was enraptured with the melancholy glottal incantations. I was learning comparative religion from life. Away from our mothers, Susan and I resolved to write an opera together, for which she would take charge of the music and I of the words. "I think I know how," I said. "You just take a good book and retell it. You mark the emotional speeches for the arias." We spent nights together, more at her house because of the serenity cultivated by her artist mother—plus, she had only two little brothers. Inside, the Gillermans' house was one big, open space of dark bricks and wood, with a fire burning in a low fireplace. Outside it lay a mini-wilderness, the wooded ridge above our school.

After dinner, Susan and I often scrambled down the hill and across the creek to the school yard, to work on our opera. We settled ourselves on the U-shaped seats of the swings, which hung on sturdy WPA chains—two girls in new saddle shoes, alone in a deserted school yard. In front of us in the twilight loomed the ghostly redbrick shape of our school, and next to it, the outlines of three oaks that seemed to grow from one trunk. Something in the darkness propelled us to swing, and we swung and swung. We pumped higher, passing through the pit of the arc, rising forward to the edge of the dark, then backward into the sky again only to pump forward to a new precipice. After a while we let the arc of the swinging subside till we were just swirling our feet in the tanbark. Around us in the dusk the low strains of our opera's overture were almost audible. Tomorrow I would sketch out the story.

First we had to touch on another subject so elusive we could broach it only with each other. "Did you see the shirt John Felder wore today?" Susie asked me out of the darkening air. "Yeah, it looked Hawaiian," I answered, "but it was okay on him." Now came the key question: "Do you still like him?" asked Susie. "I guess," I said; "Do you still like Johnny Cytron?" "I guess," she said as we swirled some more, rakishly jiggling our swing seats.

John Felder was one of those graceful kids who could catch a ball, answer a teacher's hard question, and make another person, even a girl, feel like a companion. He had slitlike eyes, thick lips, and loud tastes in clothing. Johnny Cytron was the opposite, dark and thin-lipped, his red-plaid shirts seeming to pulsate with his intensity. He had once fallen fast asleep at kindergarten nap time, and the moment had marked him forever with a touching vulnerability. They were two of the boys we'd grown up alongside, but the two who had turned into magic runes, the significance of which we barely grasped—though it seemed we were supposed to.

As sixth grade drew to a close, classmates with rathskellers invited girls and boys together to their parties. We wore party shoes without socks to such events, and the shedding of those childhood socks, the feel of patent-leather shoes digging into our bare feet, was more exciting than even the notice of Felder or Cytron. A momentous land of new sensations was opening to us in the illusory safety of the last year in our small school. But suddenly, in the midst of its unveiling, I stopped talking about the two Johns to Susan Gillerman. I got stomachaches before parties and stayed home. My newfound sociability faltered. A secret, scary thing was happening in our house at night.

THROUGH THE WALL of my bedroom I heard my father sobbing. I heard it only once or twice at first, so I thought I must be dreaming. I had moved back upstairs to the small "sewing room" that had been the babies' room, a room just big enough for a bed under a window that looked out over the brick terrace and the big oak tree. With this new arrangement my mother acknowledged my status as almost grown, and signaled the end of babies for the family. My two brothers now shared one of the garage bedrooms downstairs; little Mardy slept in the other, the one I'd been in. Faith was next to me upstairs, in the bigger room, where she could roam by day and by night be contained in a crib with bars. I would wake if she cried and sometimes met my mother in Faith's room.

I tried not to wake if I heard my father crying, though it happened more and more as school ended and summer came. I would go to bed, then start awake in the middle of the night, as if, on the other side of sleep, a curtain had gone up on a theater of darkness where you could only hear, though your eyes were wide open. Mingled with my father's racking sobs came his muffled cries, "What shall I do? What shall I do?" But mostly it was just the deep sobbing and my mother's endless murmur, "It'll be all right,

Hen, it'll be all right, it'll be all right." Sometimes I burrowed under the bedclothes. Sometimes I sat bolt upright and stopped my ears, peering out at the terrace, at the oak tree spreading its branches in the dark, at my rope ladder hanging from the branches.

My father, that tyrant, that charmer, the capricious king of our household, was falling apart; so the whole world was flipping over. Or that's what I felt in my nightly terrors. Nobody said anything in the daytime about what was happening, though pieces of dire information could be picked up if you were listening. "Well, Combs," I overheard my father say to our neighbor, "we've lost the plane, heh, heh, heh." "What plane?" I asked. "Your father and I, honey, were going to buy a little plane together," said Bill Combs. "We put some money into the commodity market. But the market isn't behaving."

It was useless to ask my father. These days he didn't hear if you spoke to him. He slammed doors more than usual when he came in and out of the house. So I started to watch him obsessively. I stationed myself near the front door when he was due home from work. I scrutinized his face under his hat when he came in. One terrible day, as he came through the door, his mouth went sideways under the hat. He was crying in the daytime, in view of anyone. I rushed upstairs and hid in my room.

A partial explanation came one night at dinner, when my father was out and my mother presided. Prosperity, she explained sadly, was the cause of the crisis. The young partners in the new firm had agreed to draw a modest salary from their initial investment. Their remaining income was to come from commissions, which were supposed to grow as investors learned how smart they were. But by 1959 there had been years of good weather, abundant crops, healthy farm subsidies. The grain silos of the Midwest were full of wheat. Prices for commodities had bottomed out and were staying low. Nothing moved. Nobody speculated. Surplus grain got shipped to Russia. The good times, it seemed, were lethal for gamblers like my father—he needed bad times to make money. With Faith's medical bills cascading in, he was terrified. This sunny boom-time might go on forever, with us poorer and poorer in the middle of it.

My mother, the economic virgin, confronted the idea of poverty. She scrutinized the grocery bills and replaced our gallons of milk from the milkman with powdered milk that you mixed with tap water. It was milk that thinned out and became bluish at the bottom of the glass. I was aesthetically outraged. We stopped buying clothes at department stores. My mother planned what clothes we needed, then took us all downtown to a hotel suite occupied twice a year by Best & Co. We tried on their samples, then received our minimal wardrobes in brown boxes through the mail. I had a loud argument with my mother in the Best suite about a red dress with white piping and a dropped waist, which she said looked cheap and I said was grown-up. In my mind it went with the powdered milk: if we're poor, let's be less proper, a little rakish. I won by default—she was too tired to argue. It was a terrible time for her, trying by night to invigorate my father, trying by day to will Faith to normalcy.

The rest of us also had our constant demands. A League of Women Voters calendar hung on the wall in the kitchen, with the days of the month blocked off in little squares. The squares were penciled over with my mother's neat notations of Boy Scout meetings, Pony Club trials, haircuts, doctors' appointments, dentists' appointments, lists of other mothers who drove carpools, and where and when to pick up each child. Driving, officiating, explaining, anguishing, my mother's maternal brightness was sadly tarnished. There's a snapshot from this time, taken on our terrace, in which she is sitting with Faith on her lap, and four-year-old Mardy stands beside them. The two little girls, both dressed in Sunday best, hold their heads together as if conversing. Ah, if only they could, implies my mother's thin smile—a smile of hope made faint by exhaustion.

Behind the scenes, grandparents were stirring as our family finances spun out of control. My father's father, his generosity congealed forever by Depression trauma, couldn't offer much. He was shoring up his New Hampshire farmhouse for a coming retirement. In the end, a rescue operation was mounted by the maternal side of our family. "Henry dinner with Dad," says my mother's note on the September 24 square of the 1959 calendar. A month later the position of sales manager at Sligo Steel was offered to my father by my grandfather Conant. After a few more tormented nights my father accepted, forfeiting his investment in his beloved small commodity firm, ending his second bid to leave the orbit of parents, and sending his gambling proclivities underground. Things quieted down. "Your father has a new job," we were told in an upbeat tone of voice.

I stopped haunting the front door in the evening. Relief let me sleep through the night. But it was sad to see that father diminished, even if he never paid attention to me. He came home from work almost meekly, lugging the fat blue Sligo catalog. While he sat with his drink in the living room, he turned the pages, memorizing illustrations of power saws and bit screws. Sometimes he fell asleep with the catalog open in his lap. Some nights he didn't bother to open it, but sat in the glassed-in dark of the family room, always with his drink, in front of the TV, grabbing his sons when they came by in a half hug, half brutal crush. He held them that way for minutes at a time, seeming to forget about them until they cried, "Dad, let me go, that hurts!"

I STARTED JUNIOR high that fall. Our junior high was brand-new—we were its first seventh grade. The grass was barely growing outside its two-story beige-brick facade, which was rescued from banality, or so its architects thought, by a metal arc soaring over the gymnasium. Along the concrete walkway to the school entrance, the saplings still had burlap bags around their roots.

I myself was strangely muffled, wandering the shiny linoleum halls, looking for my classrooms. Kids around me strode purposefully by in bright new sweaters, pleated skirts, and starched corduroys. I didn't know them. I had two skirts and two sweaters from Best's with which to face the year. My family was poor but wellborn, I kept telling myself. A mixture of shame and superiority lodged in my heart, along with simple loneliness. Part of my sixth grade had gone off to the other new junior high, including Felder and Cytron; another part, including Susan Gillerman, was here but in another homeroom. A few had gone to private school. I had landed by myself, a member of an old, exhausted race.

Throughout the fifties, young white families had been pouring out of downtown St. Louis into the county (not legally part of the city—alas for the city), laying ranch houses end-to-end over the empty farmland to the north and west of Ladue. Hence the need for two new junior highs. A chaos of kids flooded my new school—three hundred in my class alone, of whom the smartest (or so decided the mysterious powers who tracked us for college) were all Jewish, except for me. My elementary school, Little Ladue, had been split, more or less, between Jews and Protestants or Catholics. It had stood across the street from an old Jewish cemetery with the six-pointed star over the gate, where we schoolkids had waited in lines for the bus every day. The six-pointed star proclaimed an alien domain, but down the road my effulgent green country club beckoned, so the cemetery's strangeness, in my child-senses, was overshadowed by trees of an Anglo-Saxon caste. At my new junior high, though, the landscape was naked of vegetation of any caste, and the culture so new-minted I couldn't find my bearings. "Are you going to join the pep club?" someone asked me. "What's pep?"—I couldn't place the word. "You have to join the pep club," the person answered. I went along to the gym and, from one of the top bleachers, heard the pep club explained. It was about cheering for the teams. I joined.

Because my sense of belonging to that other domain of my childhood, the country club/church, had been weakened by the embarrassment of our now-shaky financial status, the me that emerged in the cliques that swirled on the junior high playing fields was a mildly cringing person, hiding a stern social arbiter inside. "I wish I had a pretty middle name like yours," I said to a new schoolmate, Adrian Rose Inselberg. I had already plebianized my first name—since fourth grade I'd been Liz, not Buff. We were sitting outside on the grass by the playing fields. "Well, what *is* yours?" she asked. "Bemis," I said. "That's awful," she said.

But the secret me exulted in the fact that a middle name like mine meant a social status beyond Adrian's wildest dreams. "If she knew who I am . . . a Bemis, a Conant . . ." I said to myself. The question was which to adopt, the family code or the peer code?

When I went to Adrian's house after school, I observed with a knowing hardness that her living room was a blur of leopard skin. I'd been told that meant lower-class. At home I about-faced to defend Annette Funicello, the Mousketeer, for wearing leopard-skin pants on a certain red cover of the Mickey Mouse Club magazine, which I subscribed to. Perhaps I should secede from my family and be socially ordinary, I thought. This social-order confusion created a longing in my brain for some kind of definition from the adults at school. I stared at the teachers; I searched their persons for clues in the shifting universe of social signals; I tried myself out as their friend.

Miss Zotos, the gym teacher with the dangling whistle and the Harpo Marx hair who walked among us as we sat cross-legged on the cold gym floor; Miss Fuller, the music teacher with the Little Eva blond curls who sat at her desk in a thicket of music stands; Mr. Fitzgerald, our cleft-chinned algebra teacher who had been a priest: they were all "cheap" in some way, not of my class. Or so I told myself, while nursing the fantasy that one of them would recognize my powers of companionship and take me home with them. I was an awkward, still-chubby twelve-year-old with new braces on my teeth, who imagined that because my family was "society," I might be attractive to my teachers. I was trying furiously to put myself on an equal footing with people who had power over me. You could say I reflected the upside-down power relations in our household, in which my father was laid low and my mother made suddenly strong because of her patience and her father's money. My unconscious solution, in the blank sea of junior high, was to try to insert myself into a teacher's life the way I had inserted myself since early childhood in my mother's. I wanted to be some other adult's confidante besides my mother's, to have a grown-up dependent on me and yet to depend on them. I wanted to reproduce my intimacy with my mother, outside the family.

As the year wore on, none of my favorite teachers made a move in my direction, though Miss Fuller smiled kindly when I found her after school and confessed my adoration. The teacher who proved the most restorative was the one who didn't mean to be, our young English teacher, Mr. Holman. This nervous and scrawny character in a seersucker suit was at his wit's end, having been subjected to so many taunts from rowdy boys that he was just marking time till the end of the year. He did this by reading Poe stories aloud. "I was sick—sick unto death with that long agony," he began without preamble as we trooped in and sat down, "and when they at length unbound me, and I was permitted to sit, I felt that my senses were leaving me. . . ." My ears opened wide. As I trembled with the nameless narrator in his Spanish dungeon, the wonder of being myself, with all my hot and secret opinions, in a new schoolroom with a window framing a banal rectangle of suburban green grass, poured into my consciousness like a balm. This sudden glimpse of literary torment eased that restless need to be a teacher's friend. I could be troubled alone; Poe had proved it. A tiny beachhead had opened up, an abstract refuge from my compulsive inner argument about social domains.

It was the world of the disordered mind. Its attractions comforted me when I ventured on Friday evenings into a milieu still more treacherous than junior high, the fortnightly dances. This obligatory rite of passage for the city's elite twelve-year-olds seemed unaffected by momentary vicissitudes such as our careering family finances. The timeless rock of good breeding stood me in good stead; I'd been invited at birth. Now that the hour of young womanhood had rolled around, money had been scraped together to buy me two outfits with the sheen of the ballroom— a black velvet jumper with a white satin blouse, and a blue velvet cap-sleeved dress. Pin curls were wound by my mother with crossed bobby pins, then fluffed out.

But I was more out of place here than at junior high. I was picked up in the carpool with Mary Institute girls, girls I'd swum with at the country club, lunched beside at the Women's Exchange, who nonetheless radiated unfamiliarity. The car door opened and lit up their curled hair and their little purses, their white gloves and their animated conversation with one another. I rode in the front, the silent, panicked partner to the courteous driving parent. When my own mother drove I was again silent. She made conversation with the backseat passengers, and they answered her with perfect manners all the way downtown to the Gothic mansion of the Women's Club, where chubby boys in suits and a sad little jazz combo playing "On Wisconsin!" awaited us.

My mother had suggested that I talk to the boys about what they might be interested in. "Do you play football?" I ventured to round-faced Eddie from Chaminade, the boys' Catholic school, as we tangled our feet in the fox-trot. "I didn't make the team," he mumbled. I hovered as much as possible on the sidelines of those dances, evading the volunteer mothers who took you by the hand and joined you to a truant boy. Carrying the secret truth of our poverty in my heart, I drifted near the three-man combo and scrutinized the red-headed drummer, who wore white socks under a skinny black suit. He was the kind I should aim at, an older man, a jazz player, poor, no doubt, and tormented. In my fantasy the drummer and I were soulmates—we were marginal. We hated the complacency of small talk.

Coming home, I would refuse to answer my mother's questions about how the dances had gone. There was a sadness to our relations then. "How're you doin', Buffer," she would ask me pensively sometimes, as if along the way we had lost each other, and it was her fault. Of course it was her fault, I protested staunchly to myself. One day, after a pep club meeting, she was late to pick me up. I stood there in the darkening afternoon, alone by the school, as a chill came into the air and self-righteousness bloomed in my heart. When our red Volkswagen bus finally pulled up, with her at the wheel, I climbed haughtily into the backseat.

She began to make restitution, leaving on my pillow a stuffed calico dog, a plastic bracelet, a Beethoven record. Christmas of 1959, she made me a red felt skirt, around the rim of which strode eight palomino horses laboriously constructed of pieces of felt glued together. Each horse had a tiny piece of black felt at the mouth, indicating a small horse smile. She'd made it in the nights after I was asleep. I could barely choke out my thanks, since I'd given up the horse craze when I passed along my pony to the girl up the lane, something I hadn't bothered to explain to her.

Nor was I the only one of her children who'd gone sullen in the family crisis. My brother Judd was roaming the neighborhood with a tough little boy named Eric who had moved in next door, a blond child with shifty eyes. Judd's old sunny friend Billy Combs had left the lane with the rest of the Combses. Baby Suzanne had been born to the Combses and another Combs was on the way, so that family had bought a mansion downtown as big as a school.

Now there was no father Bill Combs to burst into our back-door shouting "Henry!"; no mother Edmee to call my mother "doll" on the phone; no Toni Combs to share my child-care duties with. The "Wickersham News," that hand-lettered sheet of witti-cisms and tall tales, put together by Combs and Kendall boys, ceased publication. Instead, Judd stayed out after dark with Eric. Mysterious fires started up in the creek, mailboxes were rifled, a neighbor's new saplings were bent to the ground, rocks were thrown at cars. A policeman appeared one day at our door, hold-ing my big-eyed, skinny brother by the collar. "This your son, ma'am?" he asked. "He and another boy nearly caused an accident up there on Ladue Road." My mother's face turned ashen. My father, startled out of his lethargy, advanced white-hot on my brother. Judd's allowance was forfeit a year in advance to pay for the dent in a stranger's car. My mother didn't even know how to talk to him for a while, but she knew how to talk to me.

As the temple of family fell soundlessly about my mother's head, a half-conscious certainty rose from the ruins: her oldest daughter would receive, by fair means or foul, the girlhood she had had herself. My well-being would guarantee the family's own. The chance to make good on this resolve was handed to her one day, as if by magic. The Winter Olympics in Squaw Valley, Cal-ifornia, were on TV, and I was an addict. It was February 1960. I was still twelve. I rushed home daily from school to sit in front of the TV, my books flung onto the couch beside me. I shushed any-one talking around me. I burst into angry tears if my mother called me to Faith-duty. These black-and-white pictures of tiny human daredevils hurtling down the snowy slopes seemed to hold my salvation.

Then one evening my aunt Gigi, my mother's blond, adventurous sister, appeared at the doorway of the family room, all silvery in the light of the TV. She was dressed in city clothes—she'd just come from her job. Finished with college in the East, she had come home to work for a filmmaker while she kept her eye peeled for a local husband, or so thought my grandmother Biff. But Gigi wanted something grander than the local scene could cough up, and she was master of her time and her salary. She decided, for her first vacation, to take herself to that glistening land of eligible athletes, Squaw Valley. In a burst of familial intimacy, she invited her sullen niece along.

My mother embraced the plan, meeting every impediment with an ingenious new strategy. "Christ, Betty, you know we don't have the money," I heard from my father through the wall at night, followed by my mother's quiet murmurs. My father's outbursts, my mother's rebuttals—a sequence of voice tones woven through the night. She believed she could find the money via the usual cutting of corners and explaining to grandparents. She drove off to 25 Briarcliffe to talk to them, returning with a pair of her own baggy wartime ski pants and her old Vassar suitcase. I lay in bed at night in a turmoil of emotion. I didn't deserve this trip. I hadn't helped her enough. I'd been moody and impertinent. The bills from Faith's medical tests hadn't ceased coming in. And my brother Judd: I knew just why he'd thrown the rocks. Why should *I* get a ticket out of here? I listened for clues to my fate through the wall and resolved to refuse the trip in a noble gesture.

But another voice was sounding way down in my heart. "There is no justice," it said. "Take it, take the trip," it said. "If they find the money, take it." That voice grew louder as my mother gradually prevailed. It was a suddenly shy Betty who drove her fierce and heedless daughter downtown one day in March, to the Romanesque echo chamber of the old Union Station.

THE WINDOWS OF the train going west were dark all around. "Hello, hello," I said to passengers we passed in the narrow corridor outside the sleeping compartments. Somewhere in Kansas it got to be bedtime, so I asked my aunt, "Do you put me to bed?" "Are you kidding?" she answered in her cigarette voice. "You put yourself to bed. But let's go talk to the brakeman first." The brakeman in the last car, a big man in overalls, told his rapt audience of two that he knew every inch of these rails from Kansas City to San Francisco—"Every dip and rise of the land, every tree, every blade of grass. If you set me down in the dark anywhere along here," he said, "I'd know exactly where I was. Excuse me, folks, I have to go out and check the tracks."

He took his lantern and disappeared out on the ramp at the end of the train, into the starry night. We made our way back through swaying corridors to our compartment and went to bed. I woke in the night and pressed my face to the window. It seemed the blue dark rushing past outside had come into my body, under my skin. When you've lost something and you don't know what it is, you keep looking all around for that thing, because you feel that it might be lonely for *you*. I'd lost the part of myself that fit into the family, and I was on my own in the immensity.

Chapter 6

....

W ITH THAT TRIP BEGAN THE PATTERN OF THE REST of my mother's and my joint life: I was the prodigal, venturing out and coming back in ever-widening circles, always looking for something—escape from her? Reunion with her? The two were strangely similar. In Squaw Valley, rather than turning into the glittering cosmopolite I had assumed the setting would make me, I became a crabbed version of my mother. "Why do you want cigarettes from that man when you have cigarettes in your pocket?" I asked my pretty blond aunt as we skied to a stop on a snowy cliff beside a Frenchman from our lodge. I interrupted her flirting; I hid her cigarettes to stop her smoking; I offered to pay back people who took us to lunch; I got stern and doubtful when she brought us to a theater in San Francisco where modern dancers gyrated on a misty stage. Maybe it was my mother's clothes that held me in thrall: those dark, baggy ski pants set me sadly apart from the figures around me in their peacock-hued second skins (Lycra had just been born in the ski world).

It wasn't until I got to summer camp that I found the release from the family that I seemed to crave. That came in June, only two months after my glamorous, confusing ski trip. Crisscrossing the country was an extravagant proposition for the daughter of a near-bankrupt family, but camp plans for me had been put in place before the Squaw Valley trip. Besides, camp seemed to be one of those things you just did at my age, like the fortnightly dances. It was the other side of the coin from the dances: if they were supposed to train the manners, camp was supposed to train the soul—and the soul would sustain you through all the trials-by-manners of later years.

That's what my grandmother Biff gave me to understand as she sat at the piano and told me about Pinelands. She had loved her New Hampshire camp, with its cold, deep lake and fir trees on the hill. My mother, too, in the years before the war, had been Pinelands's best swimmer, second-best canoer, and the Head Elf in a famous 1941 *Midsummer Night's Dream* performed in a glade. Deep inside she had retained a glow of Pinelands: you could see it when she put on her bathing cap and swam a few sedate laps in the country club pool, as if, once dipped in that northern air, she could never wither or age. But Pinelands wasn't there anymore. After the summer of 1941 it had silently folded its tents; so a new camp was found, in Vermont, with the improbable name of Aloha—a salute, said its brochure, to its founder's missionary childhood in Hawaii.

I went off to this Aloha in a state of reckless passivity. A snapshot from Easter, 1960, between my two trips, shows us five kids grouped in our Sunday best on some brick steps in back of our house. All are smiling up at the photographer (my mother), except Faith, in the front, wearing a pinafore and looking distractedly down; and me, at the back, in a madras shirtwaist and staring bitterly ahead. I'd been raging and sobbing at my mother for photographing what I called a "fake moment." Getting on a plane to Boston by myself, however, shocked me into partial calm. The sight of the camp from my Kendall grandparents' station wagon—they'd collected me and driven me up—calmed me more: a mountain clearing, some tents, mist on the ground, a white gabled house, a porch filled with girls in green shorts and white shirts. We pulled up to the house. I stepped out of the car into a crowd of eager counselors. And I vanished from my old self, through a curtain of green.

ALOHA OCCUPIED A steep meadow that descended to the shore of a middle-sized lake called Morey and ascended partway up a little round wooded mountain called Winships. Strewn on this mountain face were tents, cabins, stone fireplaces, and a couple of grander structures: the white farmhouse on the road, where the sainted Gulick family had first welcomed a handful of hardy girls in 1905; and a dark wood assembly hall down on the waterfront across the road, built in 1920s New England rustic (a close cousin of Adirondack style). It was called the *Hale,* which means "house" in Hawaiian. A hundred girls and women filled these premises for eight weeks: girls of thirteen and up (their younger sisters went to Aloha's junior camp on another lake), counselors of college age, and the handful of older directors, including Mrs. Helen Gulick King of the little white sneakers and soft white hair, the last surviving member of the founding family.

I was in a cabin at the top of the meadow, with a sensible, blond senior counselor from Wheaton College, a dizzy, red-haired junior counselor from UMass., and four girls of thirteen as wary and awkward as I was—all of whom I entrusted, at once, with the familial heart my own family had lately lost.

I offered my heart, actually, to the whole of Aloha, and as the summer wore on, it was accepted. Counselors who weren't mine started to beam at me when they thought I wasn't looking. Campers, most of whom were older, since my age group was the youngest, invited me to sit on rocks for consultations. I got a reputation for saying earnest, helpful things with a zing, an aftershock of surprise because I'd divined so much. My counselor equated my desirability with "unusual spiritual maturity" in her end-of-the-summer letter to my parents. It was more an instinctive response to girls, something like a sixth sense. I'd been used to gauging my mother's mood since early childhood and altering my energy accordingly. Here everyone was an aspiring mother. I just responded to them, joyfully or thoughtfully, depending on who approached me.

I knew my own game. One day as I sat cross-legged on the lake dock, spinning out some doubts about God to a pixie-haired swimming counselor so she could practice her mothering, I noticed the lake water winking, as if nature itself was on to me. The counselor didn't see; she was pondering my loss of faith. But I, too, played counselor with furrowed brow if some camper came to me with her earnest doubts. With counselors I was daughter; with campers I was mother. I was everywhere—playing, like a musician, on the hundred-valve organ that was the camp population. One chill morning I woke before reveille and took the dirt path to the bathroom shack; a stab of happiness pierced me to the core. The lake gleamed pink below. Around me, exposed by rolled-up tent sides, slept girls—a dark head here, an arm dangling there—who would shortly wake up to the feast of communication.

It wasn't just the mothering and daughtering that thrilled me, it was something masculine that I was breathing in as well, something I hadn't even known I'd missed: the outdoors. At home in our household, the world had been sliced in two. My father got the outdoors, along with passions, sensations, and images. My mother got the indoors, and reason, justice, kindness—colorless virtues that could be appealed to in a pinch. At Aloha there was plenty of exposure to the colorless virtues. In morning assembly, one of the older directors stood by the *Hale*'s flagstone fireplace, her knees wrinkled beneath her green shorts, and exhorted us in homespun style to be kind, generous, and selfless.

But the lake water always rippled behind us as we sat on the polished floor; pine forest smells drifted in; green grass showed through the glass door in front. The outdoors infused the sermons—it stole into the very words. One morning a shy counselor in a red-plaid shirt rose to speak. "Build of your imaginings a bower in the wilderness," she intoned, consulting a parchment-colored book, "ere you build a house within the city walls. . . . Your house is your larger body. . . . Does not your house dream, and dreaming, leave the city for grove or hilltop?"

What was that little book? *The Prophet,* that mystical text written in the 1920s. On the front, a man's oval face floated in a mottled background. Inside, topics like Beauty, Friendship, Pleasure—everything that waited for us in the land of grown-ups—were decked out in nature pictures.

Here was a society of women insisting on reason, justice, and kindness, but planted in a man's outdoors, the same outdoors I'd known every summer at my grandparents' farm, the same sharp air, the same leafy woods, the same mountains that turned blue in the twilight. Only now it was mine. It came through my cabin window at night, onto my face, unimpeded by screen or glass. It got into my lungs, and I won swimming races, I bounded onto tennis courts, I wielded paddles in the backs of canoes, I led girls up and down the hill, and I sang, with all my heart, whenever the camp as a body began to sing, which was nearly all the time.

We sang songs in the middle of meals, halfway up mountain trails, huddled around campfires. We sang evenings in the *Hale,* in a great oval ringed around its polished floor, before we climbed the hill in semidarkness to our tents and cabins. We never stopped to learn the songs, we just picked them up, joining some unseen chorus that had been singing them in this place since the turn of the century, when American youth had appropriated the nature-enchantment of the English Romantic poets for their own ends. "Swinging along the open road / Swinging along under a sky of blue," we sang, à la Wordsworth, on day hikes. "The silver moon is shining / Upon the silent meadow," we sang, Keats-like, in the evenings, or "Peace, I ask of thee O Mountain, peace peace peace!" Or the last and holiest, "When the shadows lengthen on the hillside / And silence falls on lake and shore / Gather we to sing to dear Aloha. . . ."

Something happened to me in the dark *Hale* during the songs, something that pertained to my future. It was as if the bleak self I'd barely glimpsed in that future's thin air, staring out my own window beside my own washing machine, faded out of sight. The arms of other girls on my shoulders; the sight of girls mirroring me on the other side of the oval; the firelight from the flagstone fireplace; the lake air pouring in from the porch; the names of past campers stenciled on the roof panels above: all this freshened the future, or else warmed up my imaginary body within it. I was too young to understand that I was receiving, by osmosis, the spirit of early camping that sturdy Aloha had worked to keep alive. Organized camping had sprung to life in America at the end of the last century, out of a perceived double crisis in the nation's very self: the simultaneous loss of morals and wilderness.

Ernest Balch of Dartmouth College had founded the first camp, Chocorua, in 1881, after noticing "the miserable existence of wealthy adolescent boys in the summer when they must accompany their parents to fashionable resorts and fall prey to the evils of life in high society." Girls' camps had followed in 1902, when suffragist-minded educators concluded that girls could impersonate Balch's idyllic mix of ancient Greeks and Red Indians just as well as boys. In 1961 Aloha's stationery still featured a female imp with wings, playing a pipe and wearing bloomers; the camp name was still printed in a typeface that referred to birch-bark carvings. I even saw a waking vision of female deities one Sunday morning during a pancake breakfast at the top of our little mountain. I came out of the forest path to the rocky summit. The counselors who had gone up earlier to cook loomed above me, haloed by campfire smoke and sunlight, bigger than life: Amazons; tribe elders.

Such moments almost hurt as camp rushed to a close. How could I live away from this tribe? Could Aloha reproduce itself in the winters, somewhere in the East, at one of those solid-sounding schools my fellow campers talked about—Milton Academy, Emma Willard School, Concord Academy? Alas, I had confused my mythical vision with narrow social convention. The population of Aloha in the early sixties still came, as it had in

1905, from the wealthy suburbs of Boston and New York and Philadelphia, with a smattering of girls from the eastern diaspora in Shaker Heights or Grosse Pointe. As the only St. Louisan that year, I had appraised the situation on the very first day and had made the decision to return to the childhood nickname I'd suppressed in public school. "I'm Buff," I declared to one and all at Aloha. It was this boarding-school-flavored "Buff" I needed to preserve.

"I *might* see you at Milton in the fall," I said rakishly to my friends as the nights grew colder. But I'd forgotten conditions back home. My family had not been in my mind at all in those eight weeks, or rather, they'd been back at the wrong end of a telescope. I was glad to get my mother's chatty, wistful letters. I was pleased when I heard her faraway voice on the phone in the whitewashed booth on the balcony of the main house. I was relieved when she called to say the family had arrived in New Hampshire, two hours north by car. But on the dread last day of camp, I was sobbing as I stood on the main house porch clinging to my cabin mates. The whole family was coming to pick me up in the Volkswagen bus, all except my father, who had gone back to his new job at home. In the distance on the lake road, a station wagon appeared, then another, and another, then our red VW bus with my mother's eager face framed in the driver's window. As it pulled into the drive, I saw her. She saw me. I sobbed harder.

MY MOTHER DIDN'T know that I'd embraced some vision of eastern high society, exactly what she'd raised me to shy away from. I didn't know that she'd made her first move, not so long before, to leave society and join the masses. It had to do with

SLARC. SLARC was the St. Louis Association for Retarded Children. It was a small-time operation, just ten years old. It met in borrowed halls like the Meatcutters' Medical Center, where my mother had gone to her first meeting on April 27, not long before I left for camp. Before that meeting the prognosis for my youngest little sister's growing up at all had been bleak indeed.

Faith was nearing three, the age when the rest of us had started preschool, along with the other stimulating pastimes like reading picture books and riding tricycles. My littlest sister still put a death grip on picture books and tore them apart. She continued to squeal or scream or keen, even when strapped upon a toilet and sung to in the vain hope that she would learn what a toilet was for. She could grab a person's hair in a second, or another child's, and hold on with mad glee. But SLARC had heard of such things. It had a few programs in place—vocational workshops and bowling evenings for older kids, a tiny pioneer preschool program for younger ones, in two churches. SLARC received my mother with all of her hurt, her exhaustion, her shame, her hopes for Faith's progress, which she had held on to against the odds. These parents could recognize the heartbreak for what it was, but they were not the people she had grown up with. They were socially modest St. Louisans from neighborhoods my mother had never been in, with a sprinkling of Jews and a preponderance of what was vulgarly known as "scruffy Dutch"—the old German stock of St. Louis, who had brought with them, from the exodus of 1848, a firm belief in social reform.

"Bring cake to retard office," says one of the squares on my mother's wall calendar in mid-May. That's when she jumped in, helping with a bake sale, driving out to pick up some retarded preschoolers when their bus broke down. Even such small gestures lightened my mother's action-hungry heart as we went off to New Hampshire on our annual trek. There, coincidentally, new summer arrangements had given her sudden autonomy within the extended family. Until then we'd spent every summer with the grandparents in their farmhouse on a hill, where our childish demeanors came under scrutiny and, by implication, my mother's newfangled mothering. "You don't say 'I hate peas,' " Granny had drawled to each new toddler in turn at the old pine table in the dining room, "you say, 'I don't care for peas.' " Or, "You don't just slink out of your chair, you ask 'May I please be excused from the table?' " In 1958, alarmed by our sheer numbers and our smallest sister's raucousness, the grandparents had built an elaborate fishing camp for themselves on a nearby lake called Martin Meadow Pond, where they planned to retreat in the summers. But we had followed them there, a daily mass of splashing bodies on their half-moon beach, so they retired to their farmhouse and left us the mini-cathedral of wood and glass on the lakeshore, buried in dense green woods. That's where we drove from Aloha that summer of 1960.

Our own house! The calm inside was palpable, even to me in my postcamp numbness. Not only were the grandparents gone, but my father was too. A routine had arisen in his absence, and in mine. In the mornings my mother and my brother Judd knelt to light the fire on the hearth, their dark heads side by side. My littler siblings paraded proudly to the kitchen with their cereal bowls and put them in the sink. Baby Faith flung spoons of cereal from her high chair to a chorus of easy laughter. My mother, in Bermuda shorts, looked like a girl again as she peered around the kitchen's swinging door to call us all to the table.

That summer marked the birth of a family-within-the-family, a semiconscious guerrilla unit manned by children and headed by a mother, that was to flourish under my grandparents' and my father's noses until my mother's death. It was a kind of freemasonry dedicated to "naturalness" with no affectations, to harmony with no tantrums, to unchecked silliness and robust family projects like climbing mountains. Coming in late, with my own ideas of such things devised at camp, I found myself half in, half out. In those first days after Aloha I hunched fiercely over a book on the grandparents' raw-silk couch. The other kids left me alone. They tiptoed around me. If we went somewhere in the car, they ignored my sudden bouts of sobbing, my suffering mask affixed to the window. When I about-faced and joined the talk as if I'd never left, they accepted it, but warily. They seemed to think my reappearance in a position of prominence derived from some weakness of my mother's that they should humor.

In fact, adolescent inner turmoil and the emotional blaze of Aloha had put me beyond the perfect allegiance they were acting out in that strangely free and rustic house. One twilight I showed up in a desperate mood in the small kitchen, where my mother was washing dishes with the door open to the tanbark and the woods beyond. "Mom," I said nervously, "I've been thinking hard. I think," and here I started crying, "that I should go to boarding school. I hate junior high," I sobbed.

"Oh," said my mother, and I saw in her shocked look just how much I'd presumed on the family finances, and on her own affections. Then her expression softened. "Not boarding school," she said, "we could never afford that. And anyway, how could I let you go?" She smiled sadly. "But," she added, "maybe private school at home. Maybe Nonny and Granddaddy would help."

Hidden in my mother's longtime assumption that I was her twin, heading with her toward a family utopia, was her need to see me as the fresher, untarnished twin, a better, newer version of herself. She'd persisted in this view even through my chubby period. But now, with new doubts plaguing me and inexplicable miseries and retrograde tendencies, what was she to do? And my growth struggle wasn't all that was happening in the family. Faith, as she failed to develop, was also transforming those familial depths where my mother's self and our communal selves were one.

To a religious temperament like my mother's, Faith's condition had clear symbolic implications. "Suffer the little children to come unto me," Jesus had said. "Blessed are the meek, for they shall inherit the earth." Faith, a shell of a child, dumber than meek, was a sign from God, which meant my mother herself had been chosen. That summer, standing on the lakeshore, balancing this naked, wild creature on her hip, my mother looked as if she'd been purged of the chronic anxiety that had dogged her in her marriage. Who knows what reserves of humility and resolve Faith had awakened in her? As our mother changed, so the family— previously pitched toward the bright progress of "normal" children, with me and my school projects and my childish ideas in the lead—was turning toward Faith. It was embracing the wordless conviction that our excellence, our accomplishments, our success had a higher purpose: to shelter this half-human creature and others like her.

Back home that fall our house took on a missionary tinge. Small retarded kids, with nervous parents hovering, came on the weekends to "play" with Faith, to career with her in concentric circles. We were kind to them. Flyers, envelopes, rolls of stamps appeared on the dining room table, and children were put to work stuffing and stamping. Facts and figures about re-

tardation were bandied about. "Three out of every hundred babies born in our community are mentally retarded!" "One in ten
families in the nation is affected!" We could spout these statistics
on command.

I was caught up, even in the midst of such crusading, in the
high drama of choosing a prep school. My mother had asked the
grandparents; they had agreed to help. I weathered all-Saturday
exams in the half-empty study halls of the two private schools
that stood like bookends on the two sides of the country club
grounds. On the east was the coed John Burroughs, a sprawling
old building of ivy-covered stucco; on the west was the all-girls
Mary Institute, a new redbrick, neo-Georgian temple. Burroughs
stood for student government, for comfortable old tweeds, for
the United Nations; Mary I. stood for debutante balls and polo
games and a strong presence in the Junior League. Both accepted
me for the following fall, both with some reservations about
what Mary I. called "an original turn of mind doing the work of
solid preparation." I was supposed to choose Burroughs, my
mother's alma mater. My grandmother Biff had chosen it a generation before for my mother, rejecting her own Mary Institute as
too social.

But I chose Mary I. How could I help it? I'd grown up eyeing
it from our church. I'd been taunted at fortnightlies by its demoi-
selles. With Aloha in my heart, I was ready to take it on, to have it
take me in. Its school blazers, after all, were Aloha-green.

And then I went numb. I sleepwalked. A new identity waited;
I could displace present anguish (failing to do the splits in cheerleader tryouts) onto the future. "I don't need to be a cheerleader;
private schools don't have them." Only a jumble of impressions
remain from that interim year, 1960–61, before I started the new

school. In one of them I'm standing against a row of lockers in my junior high, tearfully defending Nixon to a bunch of jeering Kennedyites. My parents, in one of their last obedient gestures to their parents, were voting for Nixon in the November election—the only parents to do this in the whole school.

In another memory that seems to contradict the first, I'm sitting in a pew with my mother and brother Judd in a close-packed Negro church downtown, a scary neighborhood where we've never been. My mother has brought us to hear a young minister named Martin Luther King Jr., whose thinking, she says, is bold and new. But our white faces are shining obscenely in the charged and crowded darkness. Or that's what I feel; my brother has no such qualms. As the scaffolding of rhetoric rises higher and higher, as King's jack-o'-lantern face with the thin tracing of mustache holds all eyes, my brother marches to the podium, small and straight in his first suit, and reaches up a crumpled bill. "Brother Kendall, a little white boy," booms out a dark-skinned man next to King—it was Ralph Abernathy—"giving his life savings of ten dollars to the cause. Open your wallets, you folks!" Friendly laughter breaks out around us.

My mother and father both had paid vague, sympathetic attention to the 1950's reports of King's southern bus boycott and sit-ins. They saw themselves as a liberal young couple. But as time wore on, my mother found in the young minister's work something she desperately needed for herself: an echo of her private religion, which included a longing to help, to shelter, to simply love the people vastly different from herself who needed her, not the people she'd grown up with, whose needs were submerged in hearty manners. So she had ventured forth like a stealthy lover, taking us two as companions, to a neighborhood where no white people went. She, too, was caught in an old life, not knowing how to break free, not knowing where a new one could be found.

The domestic catastrophes that had struck our family, the one-two punch of near bankruptcy and retardation, had knocked both my parents so severely off course that they were drifting, rudderless, among several possible lives. And youthful components of their personalities were rising to the surface. My mother was becoming again the college girl who had wanted to "sway the whole college in a mass meeting." My father, enmeshed in subservient familial bonds at Sligo Steel, was forging yet another escape in his off-hours at home, the telescope forgotten. He was finding a way back to his lonely childhood when his mother had gone to work in the department store; he had consoled himself with birds.

The first hawk appeared in our yard that winter of 1960–61, a gray goshawk wearing a leather hood with a plume and sitting on a perch. Its beak was pursed in an expression of steely patience curiously like my father's own; its feathers were speckled like a hand-knit sweater. I admired the bird. So did my father. He often lifted it on his gauntleted wrist and gazed at it. Sometimes he brought it indoors on his wrist, attracting a trail of openmouthed neighborhood kids. When he halted with the bird in the living room, near the piano, the effect was striking. On the piano stood another symbol of the wilderness: a glass aquarium, housing a young boa constrictor bestowed by the same boyhood friend who had given my father the hawk. The boa was George, our new household pet. It writhed and coiled around in an environment of gray twigs; it had a skin as speckled as hawk feathers, but curiously dry to the touch; it ate one terrified mouse a week while we watched. The sight of the mouse, moving as a lump inside the snake, was the new, compulsory family spectacle, more ghoulish than the old one of the telescope lens shadow on the wall.

Then one morning the aquarium was empty. George had escaped, causing the resignation of Maidie, who hated snakes, with floods of tears all around. Maidie's husband took her suitcases out to the low-slung car that picked her up, leaving a disbelieving grief so vast that my memory hasn't recorded it. A general sensation set in, as George remained lost and Maidie gone, of a once-cozy home grown sinister. "He'll turn up," said my father of George, with a detachment I found obscene. My grief about Maidie turned to rage at him. He didn't feel anything.

George did turn up in the garage, some months later, living happily in a pool of axle grease (snakes don't need to eat often). We hardly noticed, since in the meantime something even more momentous had occurred. My mother was pregnant again. "Dad and I decided to end the family on a good note," she explained a bit plaintively to me. To her sister Dodie she confided that this baby was "for Henry—so he can feel good about himself, that he's produced a healthy baby after Faith." But as her stomach grew bigger, our house grew smaller. There was no place for another baby. A search was launched for a bigger house, a sad and wistful search, owing to the money. "Maybe we'll be a rural family! Maybe we'll be royalty!" I thought dreamily in the back of the car, as we viewed sprawling villas in the country and stern mansions in the city.

The house hunt seemed hopeless—they were all so expensive. Then my father met an old schoolmate at a party who told him about a place for sale not far from us, a large house on five acres that everyone had forgotten about—it was cheap thanks to near dereliction. Brambles hid it from view. Snow and rain came through its roof. An elderly widow lived in one wing of it with only a maid for company. She never went out: her groceries were delivered. "The old Stannard house," mused my paternal grandparents. "It was grand." "You can't buy that monstrosity—nobody could fix it," said my maternal grandfather, sucking on his pipe. "It's bigger than his house," my father observed drily to my mother, "that's why he doesn't want us in it." A sudden windfall from a bull market in soybeans (the commodity market was still my father's secret vice) buoyed his nerve. He bought the house, and he drove us to see it on a fecund late-spring day.

My pregnant mother had stayed home. The new baby was imminent. As our old house receded in the rearview window, we turned around and gazed at the road ahead. Almost too shadowy for anyone to know it, we four and my father comprised another family-within-a-family—a family that held out a vague and risky promise of adventure, of mystery, of selfishness of the spirit and exhilaration of the body. Not a family at all.

That was something of what the new house whispered to us on that faraway day when we first met up with it. The car had turned left off the county road, lurched down a half mile of rutted driveway, then turned a sharp right to find the long, crumbling, yet still symmetrical structure of white brick reposing in an island of fantastic underbrush. It had a colonnade over the front door, two stories of tall windows with flaking blue shutters, a sloping roof of broken tiles enlivened by an eyebrow window in the very middle. Huge old trees arched above the house. Vines laced among the trees shut it off in eerie silence. The ground behind it sloped away.

As my father stood on the driveway surveying his new domain, my twelve-year-old brother Judd took off down the slope of waist-high grass and thistles behind the house and vanished. We saw him in the air, attached to a vine, and heard his cry when he dropped to the ground. Harry, almost eight, a crew-cut little boy of intense sweetness, took off after Judd and stopped short at a hump in the undergrowth. "A fort!" he called out, and pulled up some branches to show a semicircular stone bench. Mardy, a delicate, blond six-year-old who was usually scared of everything, tried to follow Harry through the tall grass and brambles. She floundered and stopped, but as she turned her head up toward a corner of the house where some bees buzzed against the sun, a smile of delight crossed her face.

I stood still and watched the others, paralyzed by all the impulses welling up in me: I wanted to jump up and down, cry tears of joy, scream, shout. I started running, tearing through brambles, oblivious to scratches. I ran around in back of the house down a hill, toward a field I'd been told I could cut through to my new school. There was more yard than I'd ever seen. At the bottom of the slope I looked back up at the house. Two stories of columned veranda stretched across the back facade.

It was majestic; it was grand; it was Tara from *Gone With the Wind*. It was a setting worthy of a private school student. Yet something else tugged at my mind about why the house was right: it was half ruined, and that fit the family.

Chapter 7

I F I AND MY FATHER AND SIBLINGS WELCOMED OUR falling-down new house, my mother at first almost feared it. She had loved our old house on Wickersham Lane. It was so neighborly, staring brightly over suburbia from its plot of high ground. The new house was cut off from the world, haughty and self-sufficient. It must have looked to her like a symbol of the old local aristocracy she wanted, at least partly, to disown. Besides, disaster waited inside: linoleum heaved off the kitchen floors; the upstairs porch was rotting out; heating pipes groaned behind the walls; the dining room wallpaper hung in tatters.

To complicate matters, my new baby brother arrived on moving day, June 1, 1961, at the moment of suspension between two houses. I remember the scene in our new driveway. One minute my mother was bent down marking cartons, the next she stood up and shouted to my father to take her to the hospital. They drove off; the rest of us clung together by the front door open to rooms unknown. I was in charge. My panic focused on the empty kitchen cupboards. What would we eat? A few days later, mother and new baby returned to an indoor panorama of upended furniture and half-opened boxes; of children scared of the dark, searching for clothes, clamoring to go to the pool, to friends' houses, to the airport on time (that was me: I went back to Aloha soon after we moved).

The house was still in chaos when I got home from camp, but my mother had changed. Instead of hysteria, what welled up in her as she contemplated the wreckage was an involuntary gaiety. You could stick your head into the dark dressing room where she was nursing baby Sam and get her cheerful advice on anything. You could hear her drumming tunes with her knuckles on the wall as she went up and down the stairs. She laughed about the dining room wallpaper: "If you each take a loose strip off when you walk through," she told us, "the walls will get scraped by themselves." It was as if she'd been released, suddenly, from the laws of good grooming.

What cheered her most was having Faith in the middle of everybody. In the old house Faith had been stuck at the end of the upstairs hall. Here she was central: all our rooms opened out, or down, on hers, the first on the left as you came up the stairs. The doorway was gated; you could see through it to the high-ceilinged sweep of space, the French door to the porch, and Faith's small silhouette shuffling among the mangled toys. When she heard us dashing up and down the stairs, she would shuffle over to the gated doorway. We would stop and talk to her, or pat her over the gate, or pick her up.

*Corporal Judson Conant,
U.S. Marine Corps. Died in
action, Okinawa, 1945.*

*Betty and little sisters
Gigi (left) and Jane, in
Briarcliffe, winter 1945–46.*

ST. LOUIS POST-DISPATCH   PAGE 3G

LT. COL. AND MRS. SAMUEL
DOZIER CONANT and their
daughter, MISS ELIZABETH

*Betty and
her parents,
wartime.*

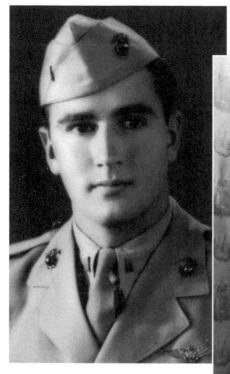

*First Lieutenant Henry Kendall,
U.S. Marine Air Corps.*

*Helen (Dodie) Conant, Betty's sister,
photographed in the Conants' front hall
as Veiled Prophet Queen, 1948.*

*Henry and Betty, off on their honeymoon,
July 1946.*

Betty and baby Buff, summer 1947.

Granny and Gramp Kendall with baby Buff, fall 1947.

Buff and baby Judd, spring 1950.

Betty with Buff, Judd, and chicken, c. 1952.

Buff (left) at the Vassar Summer Institute, 1952, with unidentified mothers and child.

Henry and Buff at home, c. 1953.

Henry, Buff, Judd, and baby Harry, summer 1954.

*Judd and Buff, in costume for a charity function, with grandmothers
Kendall (left) and Conant, November 1954.*

Above: Betty, Judd, Buff, and baby Harry,
summer 1954.
Above, right: First Nativity scene, winter
1954: Harry, Buff, Judd, and baby Mardy.
Right: Maidie McCurry, summer1957.
Below: Christmas photo, 1957.

Betty and Buff saying grace, February 1958.

Easter photo, 1959, at the Conants': (back row, left to right) Nonny, Faith, Jane, Aunt Junie, Betty, Eileen Carothers, Dodie Conant Carothers; (middle row) Gigi, Judd, Buff; (front) Harry, Stukey Carothers.

Betty, Mardy, and Faith, May 1959.

Buff at Aloha Camp, summer 1960.

New Hampshire lake house, 1960.

Buff dressed for fortnightly dance, winter 1960.

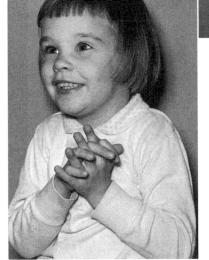

Faith, c. 1961.

Betty, c. 1961.

Mary Institute leaves for France, summer 1964: Buff is fifth from left.

The family, late summer 1965: Buff, Judd, Betty, Faith, Sam, Henry, Mardy, Harry, and dog Pepper.

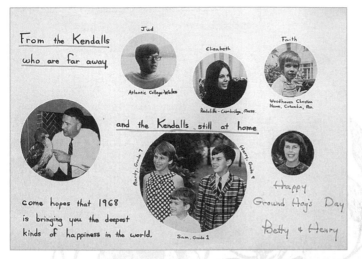

From the Kendalls who are far away

Jud
Atlantic College-Wales

Elizabeth
Radcliffe - Cambridge, Mass.

Faith
Woodhaven Christian Home, Columbia, Mo.

and the Kendalls still at home

Mardy, Grade 7

Harry, Grade 9

Sam, Grade 1

come hopes that 1968 is bringing you the deepest kinds of happiness in the world.

Happy Ground Hog's Day
Betty & Henry

The family, Christmas 1967 (card sent late—on Groundhog Day).

Betty at Fair Housing benefit, January 1968.

By Lynn T. Spence, a Post-Dispatch Photographer
Mrs. Henry C. Kendall (left) served as chairman of the benefit with Mrs. H. C. Duges. From left, Mrs. Leslie Bond, cochairman of the honorary sponsors committee, Mrs. Arthur Holly Compton and Mrs. Samuel D. Conant discuss the work of Freedom of Residence, a group dedicated to equality of opportunity in housing.

Elizabeth and Mardy with Mstislav Rostropovich, April 1969, after the accident.

After the accident, 1969–70.

Judd

Harry

Mardy

Sam

Elizabeth

Visit to Faith,
spring 1969:
Sam, Mardy,
Faith, and Harry.

*Elizabeth doing a handstand
in Death Valley, California,
spring 1970.*

*Last picture of Betty, 1969,
taken by Elizabeth and
developed after the accident.*

The house made sense of Faith—a small ruin ricocheting in a larger one. It made sense of all of us and our autonomous urges: little Mardy in the room next to Faith's, arranging family tableaux in her dollhouse; Judd and Harry kneeling among plastic soldiers in their new mock ship's cabin in the attic; me across the hall from Faith in my lavish new room, propped on my bed with a book about Russia (the most faraway place I knew); my father out-doors, orbiting in his Tyrolean hat, clearing the underbrush with pickax and crowbar and wheelbarrow. Or else he was indoors, still in his city hat and coat from the office, fussing over the "fine old mahogany pieces" that his parents had released from storage for our majestic new living room. This was no longer family as the strained organism that Vassar had prescribed, but family as galaxy: everyone shooting out from a communal center, exploding with hobbies, erupting with demands, yet absorbing deep down the new and spacious proportions.

As if to bless these very proportions, our household goddess, Maidie, returned in October 1961 to resume her place in our lives, though just on weekends. My mother must have called her in desperation. A procession of "hired help" had started brightly to work and left in disbelief after several days. A German lady named Josephine had screamed at Judd and me when we fought. "The children of the bourgeoisie don't behave like that!" Maidie took possession of three tiny servants' rooms above the kitchen; her presence transformed those rooms, as well as the kitchen below, and the laundry room and pantry with their old checker-board floors of black and green. When the back door off the kitchen was opened on the weeds outside, their vegetable green blended with Maidie's cinnamon-colored figure at the stove, her indulgent smile behind her gold horn-rims, to give the impression of ancient rural forces grounding our lives.

Maidie's return freed my mother to work again for SLARC, and it was SLARC that showed her, as in a mirror, the new image of herself that the house had created. Members who came to our house for meetings frankly gaped, even when my mother set them at ease with funny stories about the boiler bursting on Christmas morning. It wasn't only the facade that impressed them. The living room, with the massive old Oriental rug rescued from the widow's family, dwarfed everyone with its scale. People sat on the couch as if moored in a sea of Persian beasts and flowers. From their reactions it dawned on my mother that the social standing she had thought was inside her—something to live down or atone for—might really be outside, a structure that she could step in and out of, like the house itself.

It was the house that began to unyoke my mother from the guilt of an imperfect marriage, that gave her the first sensation of a self separate from the family. The bold idea arose in my mother's mind that *she* might be the one who could do for SLARC what no one else could: hoist it up to the charity big time. Letters flowed from her pen, homey and impassioned. "Dear Mr. Olin," went one to a local CEO, "my father, Sam Conant, has mentioned to you that Henry and I are rather deeply involved in work for mentally retarded . . ." "Dear Mrs. Shriver," went another, to the President's sister, "I am the mother of the brood in the enclosed picture [us on the grass, with the house in back], and because the second child to the left is mentally retarded, my husband and I are up to our ears in work . . ." That one invited Eunice Kennedy Shriver, who was Kennedy's main adviser on mental retardation, to speak at a SLARC luncheon and give the locals a "shot in the arm." Mrs. Shriver wrote back: "I've just read your warm, spontaneous letter . . ." and said she'd try to come.

In this manner my mother stumbled on the pragmatism within privilege: to civic fathers she played the respectful daughter; to Kennedys she played mother of a brood; to newspapers she was the society matron with a noble civic agenda. In March 1962 the *Globe Democrat,* the city's other big daily, fell to her campaign and ran its first SLARC feature, a full page of photos entitled "Retarded Children Benefit from Volunteer Efforts." No retarded child was in sight: the pictures showed country club wives carefully drinking coffee with SLARC's white-haired female founders and its young Jewish matrons—incompatible populations, if it weren't for my mother's deft social engineering. She herself perched, laughing and slim, on the arm of a couch above two flower-hatted older ladies who balefully clutched their coffee cups.

It wasn't only SLARC that had brought my mother out of herself. She had recently joined a little club of her friends, other country club wives, called AFTIOTHMS, The Association For The Improvement Of The Housewives' Mind(s). It had started as a lark, a joke, an excuse for company. But its meetings swept up its members in the startling realization that they had spent their adult lives in something like loneliness.

Those eight or nine women faithfully came to one another's houses once a month at noon, each bringing a homemade sandwich. "I was desperate to talk to grown-ups," explained its founder, Dotsie Shapleigh, the wife of our family doctor and mother of four. "We needed each other," another member wailed. AFTIOTHMS started in the fall of 1960 and lasted a decade. It was a textbook illustration of what Betty Friedan was to describe three years later in *The Feminine Mystique:* a near-mystical coming together of housewives across the land to reclaim brains dulled by baby talk. Because of SLARC and her own eager temperament, my mother's brain was in better working order than the others', at least on the surface. She harangued them about the rights of "every single member of society to live to his full potential, even the damaged ones"; she put them to work while they talked, addressing SLARC fund-raising envelopes; she made them join SLARC's board. She showed impatience with thoughts that began with "John says . . ." or "Taylor thinks . . ."; she wanted to hear what *they* thought. "Articulate," the members branded her, and it was high praise.

MY MOTHER'S NEW daring fell upon me like sunlight. We'd had a rapprochement anyway, because of the baby-care factory that once again consumed the family. Diapers piled up and pablum flew, as there were two babies, counting the oversized Faith; I was needed again. But I was older and competent now, and it was a lonely year in my new private school. I was dull on the hockey field and sharp in English class, the reverse of what was needed in a Mary Institute ninth grade. The communal opinion was delivered one day outside the gym by a girl named Rosalie whom I'd grown up with at the country club. "Hello, *Buffie,*" she said, with casual scorn. A gap arose between the mute and foolish me at school and the efficient helper at home. Extra grounding at home came from my new room.

It was my mother who had secured me the widow's old quarters, across the hall from Faith with an entrance hall of its own, a bathroom of veined lavender tiles, a French door onto the back porch. She had gotten it on the most-urgent-repairs list, so it also sported new mint-green walls, Chinese horse drawings framed above the twin beds, and a rolltop desk against the wall, where I sat over homework with the porch door open at leaf level among the tall trees. This profusion of space represented some compensation for my Cinderella room in the old house, the upstairs sewing room, but it also marked my new status in my mother's eyes. As she was changing, so was her image of me. I was supposed to be contemplating a life far afield of the family—or that's what she was signaling. My book about Russia, the first of a Time-Life series about foreign countries, was a Christmas gift from my mother. In those first months in the house, that book infused the atmosphere of my new room. Gold-toothed peasants built log roads in Siberia and pigtailed ballerinas sprinkled wooden floors with watering cans even as huge oak trees rustled outside my window and Missouri crows cawed in the distance.

My mother had taken to dropping by my room in the evenings. With all the rooms in the house—twenty-six, counting bathrooms and basements—there were none for her alone. Later, after Maidie died, she would claim one of the servants' rooms as a work space. Right then my room was her only refuge, a home branch of AFTIOTHMS. She lingered by the doorway after she'd checked my homework, and I was perpetually twisted around in my desk chair toward her. "You have to *out-nice* those girls at school," she said one night; she'd made up the verb herself. "You have to ignore how they look at you and *show* them how to be generous. That's what I'm trying to do with those old ladies who don't want SLARC to grow." "Why not?" I asked. "I don't know," she pondered. "Maybe they're comfortable with how things are now . . . but I'm going to jog them out of it."

"Oh, Mom," I said in a confiding burst, "you have to see this picture of Khrushchev." I opened my favorite book to the grainy 1953 shot of eight squat men in overcoats bearing the coffin of Stalin in the snow, while at the back of the picture, just an eye and half a mouth, flashed the younger face of the man who was now lording it over everyone, who banged his shoe on the U.N. podium and terrorized even *Life* magazine. "How did *he* get above Molotov and Malenkov and Beria?" I asked, casually citing names I'd memorized. "Step by step, I guess," she answered, "so no one noticed."

My mother, resolutely homey in her manner, was fueled inside by a conviction that she could attack any windmill in the world if she could figure out the approach. As that conviction grew through her work for SLARC, it was reflected quite wildly in me. Khrushchev, I thought, would be interested to meet an American girl with fresh thoughts. So would edgy, brassy Tammy Grimes, the star of *The Unsinkable Molly Brown,* whom I'd taken as a role model when I saw the Broadway show on my way to Aloha.

That's why I couldn't understand that other, abject mode my mother still fell into when my father was around. Evenings in the pantry, she and I would be setting the table and conversing. My father would pass the back window, then stamp on the doormat at the back door—and she would lose the thread of talk; her attention would shift out of my sphere. My father's moods hadn't gotten better with the years. You could never tell if he would come indoors with a mock complaint: "Sweetheart, which meeting do you have us at tonight?" Or a quip about the news: "Kennedy better watch it—that Castro is a wild man . . ." Or he'd be tight-lipped and would sit down at the dinner table, peer at the platter, and say, "Aw, Betty, come on, the meat's overcooked. I want it BLOODY!" And the fist would come down on the table. When he yelled, I no longer left the room to "rest" on the couch as I'd done when I was younger. Now I got red in the face and yelled back, "Do you remember the idea of *kindness*? Why don't you try it sometime?" But it didn't change things for my mother. "Oh, Hen," she would say in a tone of infinite disappointment. How could she still expect anything from him?

I had crossed my father off the list of people allowed into my small kingdom. Neither his scorn nor his praise mattered to me now, as mine meant nothing to him. Or so I thought, though I was suffused with shame once when I was lip-synching Molly Brown's defiant ballad in the bathroom mirror—"I'm gonna learn to read and write / I'm gonna see what there is to see!" and my father's reflection loomed quite horribly beside mine, framed in the window behind me. He was on a ladder, cleaning the gutters. In my conscious mind, I actively disagreed with my mother about my father. She kept saying that he really loved us but had a hard time expressing it, that he couldn't help himself when he yelled, that he was secretly proud of us, and so forth. I said forget it.

To his credit, my father did do some virtuous things that year: he joined the SLARC board as vice president. That meant that SLARC looked on my parents as my mother wished: as Vassar's married buddies working together for social betterment, though it was she who wrote his speeches, dialed his phone numbers, whispered first names to him at meetings. He made a giant effort on our spring vacation of 1962, taking us four older kids—my mother stayed home with the babies—to a beach cabin on the Gulf coast of Alabama, where we lived rather freely and ate raw steak. My mother must have made a bargain with him about the house; she must have agreed to move in *if* he would improve his familial behavior—and he must have promised to try.

But she had chosen to have a hysterectomy after we got back from Alabama, and that was a fatal miscalculation if she wanted him softer—or so it seemed to me from the atmosphere of secret frustration that lay between my parents. There was nothing wrong with her. She wasn't sick. When she went to the hospital, she told me that "this is the only way to really make sure you don't have another baby—and it wouldn't be fair to you kids to have another." I wasn't sure about the explanation. Nor can I understand it now, thinking back. Fertility for my mother had stood in for sensuality. And maybe for my father too. She told my youngest aunt, Jane, that Henry was nicer to her when she was pregnant. Did she want to kill, with this hysterectomy, that chronic longing in herself to be the sensual woman my physical father deserved? Was it a final negation of that failed femininity—or was it a statement of independence?

At any rate, even as my mother was emerging as the community leader she'd strived to be, she seemed to suffer an unspeakable loss in her feminine inner life, as if she were saying good-bye to an old self as the new one was being born. Her changed mood is connected in my memory to another moment a few months later, when we posed for that year's Christmas card. My newly infertile mother wanted one final nativity scene. So we all trooped down in costume to the basement, which was the only room humble enough for the occasion. I sat in for her one last time, in veil and robe, on a stool, holding in my lap naked little Sam who was pointing off in two directions (he had just learned to point). Brothers and sisters knelt as shepherds and angels in worshipful poses, except for Faith, who held a stuffed lamb and looked the other way. But the basement was a weird place to play the holy family. A wall lightbulb threw a harsh light on us; the background was in shadow.

Another image comes through from this time—of my mother in the mornings, standing at the green marble washbasin in the master bathroom and splashing water on her underarms, naked except for her cotton underpants with holes in them, because she thought buying new underwear for herself an extravagance. I would see her from the dressing room, where I went to check my school outfit in the full-length mirror. I would be twisting to see if a skirt looked okay from the back or if my butt looked too big, while behind me, reflected in the mirror, my mother would be washing herself as if she were a *thing*, not a body; as if, distracted, she didn't even feel the water.

Just about then, my father started his own outdoor "family." First he ordered an otter through the mail. He named this long wet creature with a whiskered face Johnny, from a nature idyll with otters that had just come out, *Ring of Bright Water*. I never got to know Johnny because he arrived half starved and streaked around like the speed of light, nipping people who were afraid of him. Then came two baby raccoons, fluff balls with black masks and ratlike feet, whom my father named Castro and Cuba. A new bunch of hawks and falcons followed, and they sat on perches in the grass by the sunroom, where anyone driving up to the house would see them first thing. Gos, Whitey, Sonnet, Blondie, Roma, Apollo—I could never tell them apart. They came and went, found, traded, borrowed, lost while flying. . . . My father was teaching himself falconry in the backyard, with a handful of new friends in hunting jackets and big boots and gauntlet gloves with birds atop them. My brothers hung around them. Even I came out sometimes to see a falcon "stoop" on a pigeon, then loop up and drop back down with talons unfurled to hit the fluttering bird again. "This is a dumb show of the cruel world," I thought portentously. But I didn't discuss with my father the symbolic dimension of his new hobby. The keenness of his profile at those moments, the air charged with concentration as if I didn't exist, stopped me before I spoke.

My father had woken up inside to a new level of excitement, and it seemed I was the only one who noticed the change, or the way it affected the rest of us. Among all the pieces orbiting the family galaxy—babies, SLARC, falconry, wilderness, AFTIOTHMS—I could see the dark piece that no one had named, the piece that had to do with my mother and father in private. They were letting go of each other; they were unbonding. I didn't say this to myself. But I sensed it in the combination of pity and fear, and something like boredom, that invaded me in the mornings when I watched my mother washing through the green Roman arch and felt my own body, under my pleated skirt and Shetland sweater, listening to what her body couldn't say. She still had the lines of a young figure to match her eager face, though her stomach was mottled from the babies, and marked by a bluish, vertical hysterectomy scar. I had a chubbier version of that figure, with the same little, pointy breasts and a jelly-flesh stomach that echoed her worn-out one in a ghoulish way.

We'd talked about sex and love, or rather, sex/love—they were supposed to be the same. And the subject was supposed to be transparent between us. Through my mother's progressive zeal, I had known about how people got pregnant or avoided getting pregnant since I was little. I had been walked a thousand times through what was supposed to happen: a boy would appear, in my grade or the one above, who was "sensitive," like me, and liked music and books. It would resemble a regular girl-friendship, but would grow into something more that would take care of the longings and weird feelings and shy questions.

She didn't say the rest, and neither did I: then you got married and became a multiple mother, then you were left with a used-up body that couldn't even feel. The beginning of boys and dating for me was shadowed by this pulling apart between my parents, this sense of failure, made all the more scary for its being unacknowl-edged. My mother never admitted what I suspect now: that her intimate relations with my father were strange and lifeless. If asked, she would talk about marriage in the old Vassar terms—a lifelong attempt at companionship, a sexual adjustment that lasted years. But the toxic truths under the surface had already passed to me and gone into my blood and bones.

IN TENTH GRADE the fortnightlies moved to the country club. Now there was dinner as well as dancing. I surveyed the boys like everybody else, and acted nonchalant and mysterious so I would be noticed. I even lit a cigarette one night, but that attempt at suavity ended in a fit of coughing. I could just as soon be found, though, staring out the window at the moonlit golf course, or stepping outside by myself and breathing in the night grass smells. (The shadowy putting greens, the sandtraps, aroused a powerful longing in me.) Walking to and from school—the only student in the whole school who had to walk, as I kept explaining to my mother to get her to drive me—I pondered the textures of things, like trees and asphalt and sunlight, and went sliding back and forth through time, pretending I was behind or ahead of myself on the walk. Not even Aloha in 1962, my third and last summer, could loosen that tight impulse to peel off from groups and wander on the outskirts.

Back at school a Byronic aura must have dogged my steps, because one day a notorious trio of seniors—the Susans, as we called them from their first names, or the Beatniks from their aura—approached me in the hall and invited me to a meeting of the literary magazine, *Greenleaves*. The Susans had long hair, pale, unhealthy skin, and attitudes of weary disinterest. My own classmates—who had joined the juniors and seniors in the upstairs study hall—tirelessly criticized them and the strange colors they wore (black, purple) and their knowing looks at one another behind raised desk lids. Oddly enough, our principal, Mr. Beasley, a tall, silver-haired, faintly mischievous embodiment of the Church of England who wore double-breasted suits, liked to have tea with them and praised the talks they gave in chapel that no one could understand. It was they who had tapped me on the shoulder. "Why me?" I asked them. "We've heard about you," they said. "We have a feeling about you."

For all its gleaming prosperity, for all its scrubbed students in kilts getting out of polished cars in the mornings, Mary Institute harbored a core of serious learning that dated back to its founding in 1859 by an abolitionist preacher from the East named William Greenleaf Eliot. Dr. Eliot had already started a college, Washington University, in his adopted St. Louis, when he focused on his own preadolescent daughter Mary. "The limit of [female] education should not be fixed," he wrote sternly, "by some arbitrary idea of how much a woman ought to know or how much it is safe to teach without spoiling her as a good housekeeper or a faithful drudge—the principle on which the education of a slave is conducted. . . ." By the time he founded his girls' academy, tragedy had struck and Mary Eliot was dead. But her father's enlightened vision for "her" school survived, and its centennial had just been celebrated when I joined the student body. In the spring of 1959, Eliot's grandson, Thomas Stearns Eliot, better known as T.S., had come in person from London and made a charming, mock-naive speech in the new gymnasium, in which he recalled growing up next door to Mary Institute when it was downtown, and using the facilities after hours. He proposed himself "an alumnus of the school—I will say even the one and only alumnus"— and made flattering reference to its "traditions," which had a "deeper value . . . than merely particular ways and pleasant customs."

Those traditions had escaped me in my freshman year; in my sophomore year they had begun to emit a faint glow from some teachers' rooms, like a pirate's lantern. The steadiest glow came from the room of Mr. Gerrard, a shy, lean, *English* English teacher with a delicate face and a mouthful of enthusiastic teeth. Mr. Gerrard also walked to school, swinging down Warson Road with his maroon scarf flying as I trudged catercorner down Ladue Road. That had made us comrades the year before, when he had tutored me in Latin. Now, it turned out, he was the inventor of *Greenleaves,* a title he'd taken from the founder's middle name. His second-floor classroom was the magazine's clubhouse.

The chill air from the window, always open a crack; the sponged-off blackboard; the maroon scarf folded on the window ledge next to his desk; the bulletin board behind the desk sporting quotes from his own reading; the old poster on the back wall with two yellowing Greek columns against a blue sea: these were the features of this grotto of a room, where a profound silence reigned, far from the social surf outside. We—the Susans and I and three other seniors—pulled our desk chairs up to Mr. Gerrard's desk, and he read poetry with toothy cadence and downcast eyes, half rising from his chair in excitement. "We shall not cease from exploration . . ." "Where comes my soul but from the sun?" "Icicles filled the long window / With barbaric glass . . ." "By the gate now, the moss is grown, the different mosses / Too deep to clear them away!" I looked around in wild surmise at my new friends. My body was levitating. Sensations flooded in: flashes of light, pockets of darkness, notions of delirium, and of pure, distant grief. One night I came home from a birthday party of a classmate to which the whole sophomore class went, and put pen to paper: "I can hear them and they / are laughing and singing loudly," I wrote. "But I must turn my face away . . ."

Besides its inner ministrations, poetry offered an invisible armor to wear in corridors, classrooms, and the lunchroom. Clad in poetry, one could challenge etiquette. I carried my lunch tray over to the senior table, bypassing my own class. Teachers pursed their mouths. In history class I took down my now-longer hair, bobby pin by bobby pin, when Mrs. Giesselman wouldn't call on me. The long hair meant I had crossed the line; I had left the fold and joined the rebels. This parchment-skinned old schoolmarm stopped the class, took off her glasses, and—this is how I told it to the three Susans in the hall—asked me pointedly, "Who are your friends, dear?" "Can you believe she said that?" I said.

Our attitudes of defiance were more than instinctual; they attempted categorical social resistance. It wasn't the counterculture yet, it was older, dandyish defiance—an echo of Eliotian ennui; a hint of Beat rhapsodizing; a dose of Parisian feminism from Simone de Beauvoir's *Memoirs of a Dutiful Daughter*. (St. Louis, founded by Frenchmen, always looked wistfully toward Paris.) This last book taught us specifics of how to *épater*, or stun, teachers, parents, classmates—and one another, for practice. "My father is dead," explained one of the Susans casually when I ventured downtown to spend the night in her seedy urban neighborhood. When we came in her back door her mother was alone, talking on the phone in the kitchen in a low, cracked voice. "The man my mother married would scream and throw clocks at her," Susan continued offhandedly as we climbed the stairs to her attic room. "I was twelve—the formative years, you know." She was intense and auburn-haired, with fastidious lines etched at the corners of her mouth.

And *my* suburban house attracted her and her world-weary urban clique. They exclaimed about the grounds, the animals, the birds, my damaged little sister upstairs, shuffling around her room. The downtown Susan wrote a piece about my sister for *Greenleaves*. "She was sitting on a red horse," it began, "in the middle of a room where three windows let in too much sun, the floor was bare, the walls lacked the familiar nursery pictures. . . ." Other Greenleavers came on falconry expeditions and were heard to whisper in awe, "The falcon cannot hear the falconer . . . the center cannot hold . . ." as my father aimed the traditional hoarse cries at a bird heading toward the horizon.

In March 1963, my father brought home a two-pound wolf cub with barely open eyes. He named it Peter. My new friends, kneeling on the Oriental rug, passed round Peter's mouse-colored little body. Seen through their eyes, my father swelled to interesting proportions. But I had the uncomfortable feeling, as we dashed up and down our stairs, mocking teachers, laughing rather loudly, that they didn't notice my mother. She didn't look to them like the courageous figure she really was: she looked humble and anxious in the wraparound skirts and loafers with little white socks she wore at home. "You see, *I* was born wild, like my father," I once said airily to one of the Susans on the stairs. Just then my mother appeared in the downstairs hall below, her head tilted up. Had she heard?

SLARC had gotten a little rough with my mother at about the same time that poetry was saving me. The older parents on the board had rebelled at the new guard of young parents—but sneakily, behind their backs. "And I'm supposed to be especially guilty," said my mother one night in my room, "for what they call 'attempting to run things without the authority to do so.' Can you believe it—they called up the national office [NARC] and warned against me. They even warned Mrs. Shriver." "But why?" I asked her in blank consternation. (My mother never could acknowledge an imperious streak in herself, nor would I see it for years.) "They think we want to replace their older-children's programs with ones for preschoolers," my mother answered, standing by my door in her usual place for working out hard thoughts. "But it's not true! We care just as much about their kids."

She came back to my desk and spread out the letter she'd written to the board: "I left Wednesday night's meeting sick at heart," it said, "because of the bitterness between all of us who were once motivated by the same thing . . ." Stricken, I looked up at her. They didn't know my mother like I did. She could talk to anyone, look a person in the eye and see who he or she really was. She wasn't controversial, *I* was. My hair hung long and unfettered. Purple had sprouted in my wardrobe—purple sweaters, purple kneesocks—a flaming badge of difference at Mary Institute. French words peppered my conversation. The zeitgeist had put a guitar in my hands. My first song, which I performed with long pauses to find the fingerings, was borrowed from the goddess of hope and defiance, Joan Baez: "Don't sing love songs, you'll wake my mother!" My own mother smiled ruefully on hearing it. But I had the sneaking suspicion that I had donned a uniform I didn't yet deserve; my mother was the one who should wear it.

Sometimes, though, she seemed to be trying it on—the behavior, if not the clothes. There were telltale signs. When I dashed into my parents' bedroom to borrow a scarf, I saw *Memoirs of a Dutiful Daughter* on her bedside table—a new copy, not my dog-eared one. "Do you like my bible?" I asked casually. "Parts of it," she answered guardedly. When I announced that I wanted to study Russian that summer of 1963, she got interested in communism. She wrote a letter to the Junior League magazine, which had recently published one member's paean to J. Edgar Hoover entitled "Communist Designs on Youth." My mother questioned the writer's compulsion to "protect" youth—"I would *want* my teenaged son and daughter to hear a speech of Gus Hall's [an American Communist leader], so they could judge it for themselves," she affirmed, and then reminded her fellow Junior Leaguers not to forget "the other 'isms' our fathers and brothers fought against, which are still a threat"; witness "the slave-like treatment of the natives of Angola by Portugal" and "the denial of some of our basic freedoms to the Negroes in some parts of this country. . . ." My mother was entertaining some daring thoughts. But since she didn't tell me all of them, I was convinced

I was blazing the trail and she was following. Or rather, that I had somehow been granted the chance to correct the drift of her life, her private life, at least, by what I did in mine.

There ensued a reckless foray into sex on the Gulf coast of Texas. I had been allowed to ride down there over my 1963 vacation, with my father's falconry friend Martin Schweig and his five-year-old son. I was the baby-sitter. An unattached younger man named Gary came along, too, in his white Porsche—he was a disciple of the falconer, slight of body and uncertain of chin, and worked for his father managing a restaurant. On the way back I made an evening visit in my nightgown to Gary's motel room. My body felt dewy after the beach and the shower. "You're a bad girl," he said as I struggled out from under him on the bed before things got out of hand. "I know," I said, smiling an enigmatic smile and inwardly heaving. I slipped back to my room. I wasn't a bad girl; I was just collecting sensations.

Anyway, how could I be bad when my mother was perched over my life like a cherub looking down on a Renaissance painting? There were epic scenes in the painting, boldly lit and full of action, though not dangerous (I didn't tell her about my visit to Gary's room). Yet perhaps she wanted danger for me as well as exploration. According to the script written before I was born, a script that lay between us deeper than consciousness, I was supposed to venture out beyond the borders of the known world. And what was out there if not danger, adventure, heady emotion, and another kind of sex than what she'd practiced? To round out my mother's life, I was to fly out of sight like a falcon, merge into darkness, then fly back with reports.

After my secret, scary brush with sex over spring vacation, my mother and I came into balance with each other, sort of.

When the family went to New Hampshire in the summer of 1963, I spelled my parents on the drive, having just gotten my driver's license. Then my father went back to St. Louis to his job. My brother Judd was away at camp for the first time. Faith, too, was away; she'd been left in St. Louis with a relative of Maidie's who was caring for her. Having started in the SLARC preschool class amid the family's high hopes, Faith had been dismissed for not being "quite ready," as the teacher said. My mother's despair over Faith's failure must have prompted her risky summer arrangement for Faith's care.

So my mother and I were the parents in the lake house, and the perfect companions I'd always thought we could be if left alone. After the younger kids went to bed, we sat on the porch and looked out at the lake. It was dark. She told me about the loons calling across the lake at her summer camp. Almost in the same breath, she added that she couldn't get the shooting of the Mississippi civil rights leader Medgar Evers out of her mind. "It's such a waste," she said in a grief-stricken tone. "I wonder if this march on Washington will change anything—all the people pouring into Washington right about now to protest how black people are treated. I wish you and I could be there," she said softly.

These moments, though, were fragile. They could be interrupted by anything—the baby crying, a phone call from my father, the briefest mention of Faith. Sometimes I upset the balance myself, when all I really wanted to do was sit there quietly with her. One evening I felt compelled to go alone to see the movie *The Great Escape,* which was playing in the mountain town near our lake. World War II prison camps thrilled me. My mother let me drive the VW bus by myself into town, to the miniature rialto on Main Street with its neon sign glowing against the mountains. I came back in the dark on the dirt road through the woods, gripping the wheel as the headlights flared on green leaves. It was the first time I'd driven alone at night. I parked on the tanbark clearing in front of my mother's bedroom window.

I went into the bedroom to tell her about the prisoners digging the tunnel under the Nazi camp and emptying the dirt through their trouser legs onto flower beds. She sat up in bed, blinking, shielding her eyes. "Haven't you forgotten something?" she asked. I looked out. The car headlights were still on. They were shining into her bed, freezing her in their glow.

IN HINDSIGHT I THINK THIS WAS MY MOTHER'S DARK-
est hour. She was in despair over Faith, whose dismissal from the
SLARC preschool had made the future formless again. But if my
mother was lost, she was also on the verge of being found. Even
as we sat on that dark porch in New Hampshire, events were unfolding in St. Louis that were to sweep her up and give her the ul-
timate purpose she'd been seeking ever since she'd taken her first
youthful vow to change the world. Civil rights, or the lack of
them, were erupting in our faux-genteel city.

JUDGE ORDERS SEIZURE OF 9 CORE LEADERS IN JEFFERSON BANK
SIT-IN, said the newspaper on the early September day in 1963
when we got home from New Hampshire. My mother devoured
it in the front hall even before we'd unpacked the car. The Jefferson Bank, once a ghetto bank, had moved six blocks over to the
main business district and "lost" its two black tellers. No Negroes

worked then in white-collar jobs outside of the Ville, the down-town ghetto. The St. Louis chapter of CORE, the local Congress of Racial Equality, which had been quietly pushing for jobs for blacks, gave the bank until August 30 to hire new black tellers. The bank dug in and got an injunction against demonstrations. CORE staged one anyway, two hundred strong—the resonance of which, coming only six days after Martin Luther King Jr.'s ex-ultant, heartbroken "Free at last! Free at last!" had rung out from the Lincoln Memorial, was not lost on white authorities. A cer-tain portly Judge Scott ordered the leaders' arrest in their homes at midnight, gestapo-style. That was too much for a heretofore decorous Negro community that made up 30 percent of the city's population. Black beauticians, lawyers, schoolchildren, and doc-tors turned out for the cause. There were demonstrations and marches and candlelight vigils under the windows of the down-town jail where the CORE leaders were held.

The city's hypocrisy had been revealed, at least to the victims. This once slave-holding city—barely loyal to the Union in the Civil War and host ever since to streams of black rural migrants on the way north; site of an old and cultured black middle class which had been barred from civic life through an impenetrable thicket of job and housing discrimination—had at last come face-to-face with itself. This awakening barely registered, though, in the do-main of manicured lawns and fairways where we lived, except at impromptu encounters of CEOs at the country club, where white-coated black waiters were eyed dubiously and mutterings of "Communist agitators" were addressed to martinis.

Here is where my mother began to attract attention. "Why *shouldn't* they be entitled to a fair percentage of the jobs?" she would ask in her most reasonable way, her earnest eyes magnified by her glasses. Then she would listen and parry as the civic leader in question tried to set her straight about "the facts." My mother's stubbornness extended even to the screened porch at 25 Briar-cliffe, where she had a heated discussion with her father. "I was idealistic once too," my grandfather told my mother, and removed his pipe, "but I bumped my head against a stone wall a few too many times. You can't reform the world in a hurry."

My mother was not alone in her pro-Negro position. In October 1963 all denominations of the city's liberal white clergy jumped in on the Negro side. Nuns, priests, and rabbis joined the picket lines at the bank. A letter was read in our suburban church from Missouri's young Bishop Cadigan, a friend of my mother's. "There are some of us," the letter slyly suggested, "who are in a position to employ qualified Negroes in positions of responsibility. . . ." No such person sprang up, but in a precursor to Lyndon Johnson's Head Start, a band of church wives signed on to volunteer at a new preschool in a ghetto church. My mother helped round them up, but didn't offer herself as a teacher. Besides being trapped by two toddlers at home (two-year-old Sam and six-year-old Faith), she was already looking at the race question differently. She talked about the Negroes with a certain wistfulness. She seemed to feel an imaginative link with the black community. Or maybe she'd had her fill, with Faith, of the ministering angel role. Whatever it was, events conspired that fall to bring her and the family closer to that mysterious world in our very midst.

Faith was diagnosed with tuberculosis, the disease par excellence of poor people. It was a shock when the doctor called. She had caught it during the summer, somewhere in the Ville, in the care of Maidie's relatives. Guilt and indignation showed on my mother's face when she told us about it. Why had she given in to temptation and left Faith behind when we went to New Hampshire? But what was an archaic plague like TB doing in our city? Diseases, it seemed, weren't confined to a ghetto; one part of town couldn't be cordoned off. My fourteen-year-old brother Judd had caught a mild case from Faith, but overcome it, said the doctor: he had scars on his lungs.

Then, in early November, the depth of our family's ties to the black world hit home. Maidie died of a heart attack in her apartment. We heard the news one night sobbed through the telephone by the neighborhood hired man, her stepson. Or rather, Judd and Harry heard—they were watching TV downstairs—and told the rest of us. Then my parents came home. It was like braving a cyclone, so unexpected, so destabilizing, was the effect. Maidie's funeral plunged us into the midst of Negro downtown. That funeral was doubly scary because of another death laid on top of Maidie's that same day, just before we drove down to Maidie's church. My grandfather Conant had died suddenly of a heart attack in the course of a minor operation on his colon. My mother dashed back from the frenzy at my grandmother's house just in time to gather us together for Maidie's funeral.

Would my mother become a child and start to cry about her father? That was my worry as we got out of the car. And she'd just had that fight with him on the screened porch about Negroes. In the dark and crowded ghetto church, we were again the only whites. I saw my mother's face upraised in ecstatic resolve, as if to convey to Maidie's people that we belonged here, now, as much as we belonged in the official funeral that would follow, the next day, in the great cathedral. There was a twisting of necks as we slipped into a pew. "Her father just passed," they were whispering. Somehow they'd heard.

How sternly my mother sat at the end of the pew! Not only had she lost the two adults who'd taken care of her—her father with money, Maidie with love—she was about to lose the most tremulous part of herself—Faith—and voluntarily. In the wake of Faith's school failure and illness, my parents had made the bleak decision to place her in a home. My father took his cue from my mother in decisions about Faith, though I think he agonized more about Faith than anyone knew. "It's for the good of the family," my mother protested. "The kids on either side of her aren't getting enough attention." By November she had already begun to visit possible homes for Faith, coming back distraught, with tales of children chained to dirty beds. It was unthinkable to deliver her child to such a place, especially this child, who had come to symbolize the unloved part of herself; it was also unthinkable to keep her home.

Into this quandary fell the funeral of Maidie, who was fused with Faith in our minds, having carried her endlessly all over the house. Now Maidie lay dead in an open coffin at the front of the church in her good clothes, her face strangely gray, and the preacher stood beside her to preach his child home. The gates of grief swung open. Maidie's friends and family, filing past the coffin, started to wail and scream and collapse on the ground. A few of them were our sometime extra maids, now resplendent in dark satin dresses, hats with veils, deep red lipstick. They didn't smile at us or bob their heads in the usual way. They didn't even look at us; they just let go in this frenzy of grief. "An ancient frenzy," I whispered to myself, and let go with my own violent sobs.

My mother stayed composed. She had to, with the four of us anxiously searching her face. But inside her heart, things were stirring. This funeral must have given her a startling sensation, almost a vision, of the races sobbing together side by side, the barriers of master and servant fallen away. This vision seemed to hover in my mother's mind in the months that followed. She found a retarded-children's home that seemed humane, the Woodhaven Christian Children's Home, two hours to the south; she cuddled Faith and rocked and sang to her, and Magic Markered her name on all her clothes. Maidie's ghost was palpable in the drawn-out leave-taking, or else it was my mother's buried self, the self of the nursery, where Negro voices had mingled with the voices of the family's southern ladies who felt themselves hardly better than Negroes. My mother, after all, still played the blues on the piano.

Now she talked to Faith in southern dialect and sang spirituals to her that Maidie had sung—I had no idea she knew so many spirituals. "I got shoes, you got shoes, all God's chillun got shoes. When I get to Heaven gonna put on ma shoes; gonna walk all over God's Heaven . . .": that was Faith's favorite. "Shooss? Shooss?" she would echo, looking pinched and vacant. "Mrs. Kendall has taught her daughter seventy songs," noted Woodhaven's case notes, "which Faith likes to sing, though of course she doesn't know the sense of them."

Although my mother never abandoned SLARC the way some parents did when their retarded kids left home—she served loyally on its board for the rest of her life—Faith and retardation had become for her the hourglass from which the sands of hope were running out. Integration, that heart-lifting idea of joining the races in our divided city, was the place those sands were flowing in. As Faith's departure drew near in that spring of 1964, the first Negro family slipped out of the ghetto and bought a house in our neighborhood, an event that caused a violent stir among our neighbors. In those days an astonishing 98 percent of St. Louis's Negroes were still confined to the city; only 2 percent had made it to the county, and some of those people belonged to old rural settlements. Petitions were sent around, and meetings convened at neighbors' houses about property rights. My mother was outraged. She baked a cake and took it over to the new family, the Dugases. "What an attractive woman," she said on returning. A few weeks later my mother drove Faith away to our waving and shouting of endearments. Faith could be seen through the passenger-seat window shaking a bracelet. An eerie silence settled over the upstairs. My mother came home grim but calm. She was ready to change her life.

AT LEAST THAT'S what I think happened to my mother that fall and spring. For the first time in our two lives I wasn't keeping track. Not that I wasn't proud of her and aware of something big happening in her psyche. But melodramas in anyone's psyche other than my own reached me dreamily, as if from afar. Even President Kennedy's death, which had followed so soon after Maidie's and my grandfather's—that shocking two beats of television film in which he was riding upright in the black convertible and then he fell out of sight—seemed to take place at an unreal distance. Or rather, its gravity, its horror, served only to lend an interesting darkness to what I thought was my own still-too-ordinary character. At any rate, all of my perceptions were rushing then toward the one, central question in my seventeen-year-old mind: how could I be different?

Detached from my mother and shorn of the Susans' protection when they went off to college, I wandered the halls of Mary

Institute looking for a new role to play—something less severe than what the Susans had affected, since I was alone on the barricades. Some friendly overtures had come from my classmates, who had returned from the summer transformed from a near-faceless bunch of rabid hockey players to a collection of wistful individuals. They were keeping diaries; they were plumbing the inner depths, where I, through my links with the Beatniks, was thought to have trod. Teachers even believed this. I was cast as Miranda in *The Tempest* thanks to Mrs. Dubois, our drama teacher with the short salt-and-pepper hair and the toadlike eyes. Some faraway bohemia of her youth—something about the Abbey Players—was rekindled by the sight of me. She made me the Girl, no small thing in a girls' school. Reclining in my simple white gown on the chapel stage before that tidy audience of green blazers, toying with my heap of shells, exclaiming "O the heavens!" at intervals to classmates flourishing capes and swords, I felt a Botticellian aura stealing over the future me.

But it was too tremulous to bear, this fragrant cloud of hope. In the late fall of my junior year I dove, for refuge and clarity, into the stringent atmosphere of French. Mary Institute was strong on French because of our city's French founders, whose descendants still graced the country club. There were real French speakers among the teachers, onetime brides of GIs, who said "u" with lips pursed in a kiss, and "errr" with a feline growl in the upper mouth. There was a new language lab with high white booths. There was a schoolmarm-general who kept us to the highest standards—Mademoiselle Mullins, of the little gray suits and the geriatric shoes, who had devoted her life to the French department.

Under this bombardment, the barbaric fantasyland of my early adolescence—Russia—slid away to reveal the chic and practical destination of Paris, France. It was mine alone: my mother had never been to Europe, because of the war. The more I absorbed this imaginary city of cities, the more I glimpsed escape from the homey tinges of my maternal heritage. I pursed my lips and gurgled in my upper mouth until my whole face was recast in a coquettish mode. I skipped lunch to sit alone in the sterility of the language lab while earphones beamed in intense French voices. (*Je sais ce que c'est, disait-t-il en lui frappant sur l'épaule.* That was Charles Bovary's neighbor comforting him in his grief.) I memorized improbable vocabulary words. I read grammar textbooks like novels. I scored 100 on dictations. A freak talent for languages had kicked in, the sum of my mother's compulsion to empathize with anybody in her line of vision, and my own musical ear. I was empathizing myself into another nationality.

Then Mlle. Mullins announced her crowning achievement, the Mary Institute Junior Summer Abroad, meant to enhance the study of French for girls whose parents could pay for it, with a single half scholarship for a girl whose parents could not. Thanks to that scholarship and to my own constant baby-sitting around town, I was whirled away during the summer of 1964 in the company of nine other young ladies in trench coats and cat's-eye sunglasses, and one dubious chaperone, to the other side of the globe. We drove in from Orly Airport as Parisians were setting out café chairs in the slanted sun of early morning. It was the freshest morning in the world. That sunlight fell on cobblestone streets, on sidewalks, on shops, on the rounded corners of buildings. From the streets arose the faint aroma of burnt sugar. I hardly rested in our spindly Hotel Lutetia, which stood like the prow of a ship where two streets met; I dashed out and talked to any newspaper seller, waiter, concierge, or crêperie vendor who would talk to me. I had the language, the key to the kingdom. I mouthed it, singsong—*"Bonjour, madame; au revoir, madame"*—snatching up the ritual melodies of French life for my repertoire, playing a solo concerto of language with a vast and teeming orchestra that didn't even know it was onstage.

What I got from those seven weeks of touring France was a new antidote to the suburban amnesia of my childhood world. Summer camp had disabused me of the notion that women belonged in houses. Now the very concept of a house was swallowed up in the parade of ancient communal dwellings that swam before our eyes: medieval hovels leaning into the street; high bourgeois apartment buildings forming a facade; chateaux with huge chambers and servants' quarters; grand hotels with quaint lobbies; villages climbing out of rock as if they'd been encrusted there instead of built. Here were the ancient essences of "city." My mother's discoveries of the social extremes had found a fairy-tale echo in the landscape of France. So had her social daring: in Tours, where we stopped to take courses in French, I and three other classmates who had caught the scent of perversity went on dates with some Syrians, two Lebanese, and an Algerian. *"Il ne faut pas tutoyer les Arabes,"* moaned our chaperone. "You mustn't be familiar with Arabs."

More thrilling than the fact of these chaste multicultural expeditions around town was the suggestion in the very air of France that flirtation—the certainty of one's allure as a woman—was supposed to be part of everyday life. Standing transfixed among the bins of underwear in the Prisunic, fingering the filmy

things in all the colors of the rainbow, I understood the hoax per-
petrated on me by my upbringing. There were no grown-up
women in America. Underwear back home was made of thick
white cotton affixed with the label "Lollipop." Here one wore ab-
breviated gossamer on one's private parts—and on one's feet,
sling-backs that clicked on the pavement with the sound of ur-
banity. I bought panties from the sale bin. I bought dainty shoes
from an outdoor market and caught a glimpse of myself in my
mind's eye, disappearing around corners on winged feet.

Home was far away that summer. When we flew back from
France, I left my group in New York and went to baby-sit in Maine
for a month, for a prissy family who lived on a rocky promontory.
Then I made a whirlwind trip, alone, to see colleges, dashing in
and out of New York train stations; staying with family friends in
Philadelphia and Boston; lyricizing my way through interviews at
Vassar, Swarthmore, and Radcliffe, followed from place to place
by adoring letters from my mother. "Dearest Fluff," said one of
the last ones, "it's been so long—I can't _wait_ to _see_ you!" with all
the words underlined five times.

But when I got home in the fall of 1964, my mother had
changed. She hugged me with pride, but something more was
happening. She was alight, charged up; she moved more swiftly
around the house. There were new books on her night table:
Charles Silberman's _Crisis in Black and White,_ with its bold black
italics on a white cover; James Baldwin's _Go Tell It on the Mountain,_
with an orange sun and tenements on its cover, which my mother
kept saying I should read because it was a young Negro writer's
treatment of religion, her most precious subject, and mine, she
assumed. There were new meetings that took her out at night.
Freedom of Residence—FOR—was the new cause: an interra-

cial band of citizens dedicated to helping blacks live where they wanted. Some secretly liberal real estate agents had funded it, so scared of their colleagues finding out, they had left their cash donations in a paper bag under a tree. My mother loved that hint of cloak-and-dagger. New friends from FOR dropped by our house, an assortment of women and even a man—my mother's first male friend on her own, a boisterous brown-skinned minister with a light-skinned wife. I'd never seen black people who weren't country people, like Maidie and her circle. Some of the new friends could have been white but for a faint wash of caramel poured over them and a sharp expression in the eyes, a kind of detachment. My mother was so proud to know them. Her face glowed like she was in love when she mentioned their names.

She had found a new landscape too, as electrifying to her as France was to me—or rather, an old landscape transformed. The city she had known all her life had shifted and shown her its secret: the black middle class. The discovery of this hidden tribe of kin changed everything. Maybe the jolt had come in the spring when she rang the Dugases' doorbell with her cake and confronted a lady whose skin was as white as hers; whose haircut was as pert; whose voice as warmly spiked with southern ironies; whose doctor husband (another Henry C.) seemed, in his casual disdain of "do-gooding," just like my own father. June was charmingly frank. "H.C. was so glad to get me out here into the suburbs," she told my mother on that first meeting, "away from all that 'community involvement.'" June Dugas was my mother's twin—as well as a Negro. There was even a college photo of June, my mother reported, on a bookshelf in the Dugas house, with upturned young face and long pageboy, that "could have been my double."

Or maybe the jolt to my mother had come in stages, while talking to June and her friends, while listening at the FOR meetings June brought her to. There the truth about the Ville was revealed: it really was a ghetto, like the old Jewish ghettos in the Middle Ages. There was no way to live out of it if you were black, except by a fluke, such as the Dugases' finding a suburban home seller through word of mouth. It was overcrowded, unsanitary in parts, stuffed with all classes of people, except for the patches of empty, desolate blocks cleared by "urban renewal." You were damned if you stayed in it and damned if you came out, to be turned away at restaurants, jeered at by neighbors, shamed into leaving stores. These were the basic, enormous facts of black life that no white people knew. "Oh, yes, your mother and I talked about how we had been treated as Afro-Negro Americans," June Dugas told me years later with her southern-softened understatement. "I told her about my experiences in school, in college . . . everywhere you went you ran into it."

My mother could hear hurt, even hurt camouflaged by irony or nonchalance. That was one of her gifts. Also, the conviction had persisted in her heart that she herself could make the hurt go away. But by this stage in her life, my mother was also a politician. She had learned from SLARC how to parse her salvational urges into strategies for improving things. In talks with real estate agents, dialogue groups at churches, parents' committees at schools, she offered concrete proposals, not sentiments. Freedom of Residence saw the good sense of this behavior. After a heated debate about the role of whites in the movement, they switched the chairmanship of our district from June Dugas to my mother, at June's suggestion. My mother's social position looked useful under the circumstances. But what impressed these new friends most was her ease with them.

She was quiet and alert when she listened. She had a warmth that wasn't maudlin, an indignation that wasn't loud. Nor did she glow too much, as I worried at the time: after years of struggling at SLARC, my mother had grown so used to her own naïveté that it functioned as sophistication. "I knew I could work with Betty as soon as we met," said June Dugas. "She was not strained." "That sweet smile of hers was enough to melt anyone," said another black friend, Charles Cason; he added that my mother, when he thought back, had the innocence of a little kid walking into a room, a kid who wants to meet everybody, who doesn't know she's not supposed to play with certain of the other kids.

Furthermore, her new Negro friends gave my mother back more than she'd gotten from anyone in her adult life. The bitterness that was the heritage of these privileged St. Louis blacks seemed to allow, paradoxically, for an ease with everyday banter, a breadth in everyday emotion. Notes of affection and wryness, a sense of skating over depths of pain with quick understanding— all that was balm to my mother's wounded soul. I watched her slide into a state of dewy animation with her new friends. She had tapped into the country's great drama of pain and hypocrisy, yet had found for herself, as a byproduct, a kind of social relief, an authentic warmth that Vassar had once promised would come from a marriage. Exhilaration made her happy, restless, and full of strategies.

Sometime that winter she took my aunt Ellen Conant out to lunch, the aunt who was married to my uncle George (he was really a half-cousin on my mother's side) who, following my grandfather Conant's death, had become my father's boss at Sligo

Steel. This aunt was powerful in volunteer circles and would later enter politics. They made small talk over soup, then my mother leaned forward. "I've decided to devote the rest of my life to bringing the black middle class into the mainstream," she said. "And I want you to come along." Ellen was taken aback. It was too radical a step at that time for her or her marriage; she decided to decline. "And what about Henry's position at Sligo?" she blurted out. "Won't he suffer?"

"That isn't important," said my mother. "This is."

YEARS LATER, when I learned about that lunch, sitting with Uncle George and Aunt Ellen on their vacation-home terrace above the sea, my involuntary reaction was a sort of shock. I hadn't realized the depth of my mother's commitment to civil rights, at least not then. Had she wanted to give up her family—even abolish my father's job—to work for the movement? Had she already left us in her own mind, five years before she left for good—before she died? There was no sign of this that I can remember from the winter of 1964–65. Our sprawling household ran on her improvisatory cheer. She sent kids off to school, picked us up, drove us to lessons and parties and play dates. With two of us in high school and three in grade school, lessons and parties multiplied. My mother delighted especially in little Sam, a blond four-year-old with an odd imagination, who insisted we were a family of cats, not humans, and he was our protector—Superkitty.

With my father, my mother had struck an uneasy balance. As she had entered civil rights, he had spent more time with the wolf, who had grown to be a powerful creature with silvery fur

and light-green eyes. It bounded up and down our backyard, attached by a leash to an acre-long guywire. My father and the wolf
were eerily close: when they wrestled, you couldn't tell who was
growling. But in late 1964 Peter had to be given up to a wildlife
preserve after a delegation of neighbors came calling to choke out
their rage. "You plow your field," one said, "and the mud runs
down into my driveway." (Every spring my father still rented a
tractor and plowed the field behind our house.) "Your raccoons
go into our garbage cans and strew garbage all over our yards.
Your rooster crows at five A.M.——every goddamned morning. But
that thing is worst of all," said that head neighbor, pointing out the
window at Peter. "That is not a malamute. That's a wolf. And I'm
going to report you to the authorities."

With the wolf gone, falconry again took center stage in my
father's life. Falconers visited from as far away as Pennsylvania,
bringing their birds and their wives, who needed entertaining.
My mother talked recipes with the wives. My father, in turn, nodded pleasantly to my mother's Negro visitors in the living room
as he passed through, carrying upside-down dead chickens to feed
the falcons. There was more than one double take. "You'll have to
fight for your rights, you know," he told a young black couple.
"White people won't give them up just like that." Evenings when
my mother and father went to the country club with their oldest
friends, they came home with parallel complaints. "Why are they
so obtuse about the race question?" my mother said. "Why are
they still hunting with rifles? The jerks," my father said. "Were my
parents born on different planets?" I asked myself, eyeing them
from the upstairs banister.

The family had survived, on the surface. But underneath, it
had shifted irrevocably. If my mother's life were a surreal play,

here would be the moment when the walls of the house would rise into the fly space in the wings, leaving the family exposed to the wide world and her standing in its midst, looking hungrily out. When Martin Luther King Jr. staged the great voting rights march from Selma to Montgomery in the spring of 1965, she got ready to go. She wanted to be in that throng, to open her throat and sing with a chorus of voices in the hot southern sun, "Deep in my heart / I do believe / We shall overcome. . . ." That was my mother: singing out her belief in a phalanx of people—in church, on Christmas Eve with us as fellow carolers, in political protests . . .

But she was prevented from going to Selma at the last minute by a crisis with Faith at her school. So instead of leaving, my mother created a double life at home, stealing resources from the family to feed the new and still mostly hidden purpose she'd given herself to. She made her phone calls while we were at school; she funneled stray cash to FOR; she informed the younger children that eating TV dinners on her meeting nights was *their* way of helping Negroes. When impatience overtook her, she drove out alone at night and knocked down a few of the black plaster stable boys that guarded fashionable driveways. Beyond that she didn't break the law, no matter how outraged she had become. Sometime that year my mother made peace with who she was, where she had to stay, what she had taken as her mission: to join her old and new lives together, to knit the city's twin elites into one.

Anyway, I was leaving home, so she didn't have to. I was exiting Mary Institute armed with the English prize, a volume of Ruskin, and bound for Harvard—Radcliffe—which I'd chosen over Vassar, with a half-mumbled apology to my mother about having heard the Harvard band on the streets of Cambridge, "like a call to arms." My arrogance, derived from a glorious and un-known future, knew no bounds that summer of 1965, though it was accompanied by attacks of nameless dread. I can see myself in a June twilight, laughing in a blue sundress, greeting my class-mates and their dates at my own party as our house, restored for a moment to its intended frivolity, glowed with light. In our school configuration, fixed in the sentimental mists of gradua-tion, I was the one "for whom the world would bend over back-wards," as one classmate gushed in my yearbook.

From that same evening, memory also shows me clinging ab-jectly to the arm of a certain dark-haired, thick-necked Princeton man, Ned Scharf, as I searched for a clever remark to capture his waning attention. I thought I had fallen, at last, in love, like a nor-mal girl my age. I had waited for the phone calls, and some came; I had made detours to drive by his suburban white house with the poignant red door. I had felt all the right tingles in my body. Why couldn't I be, with him, the freewheeling creature I had become at school? Why did such a blank panic take over when I had to talk to him?

I didn't know then, and wouldn't know for years, just how much my bold new self depended on my mother's presence. I was still a projection of her unspoken hopes and her unacknowledged hurts. I didn't have the presence of mind to focus on a boy—or anyone else—where love was concerned, without all my mother's anxiety about the realm of sex overpowering me. In-stead, I told myself that everything would fall into place up there in the future, when professional glory would overtake me. I was going to be a violinist, a decision based on years of lessons; the guarded approval of Mr. Vandenburg; my recent acquisition of a vibrato; and my infallible sense of pitch. I practiced the violin for hours in my room with an intent, rhapsodic expression that suited a future violinist. But dread attacked me here as well, when in the middle of the summer my grandmother took me to the symphony. A solo violinist in evening clothes skittered his bow over the strings of his instrument, and the strain of my own self-deception rose in my throat. I couldn't do that.

There was one place, though, where the future behaved as it was supposed to: at the Goodmans'. The Goodmans lived in Briarcliffe, coincidentally in my Kendall grandparents' former house. They were rich and cultured (Stanley Goodman was head of a department store chain); they spoke flawless French; they had string quartets on Sunday evenings, to which I was invited without my parents. Mr. Vandenburg, who at those parties played a weary viola to Stanley Goodman's ecstatic first violin, had spoken to them of me.

Candles lined the brick walk to the Goodmans' front door, where I had trod as a child. Candles abounded in their beige living room, reflecting off the crystal chandelier, lighting the champagne glasses, bathing the guests' faces in a civilized glow. Stanley, silver-haired and in a double-breasted suit, would address impulsive remarks to me such as, "There are two kinds of people, don't you think? The ones who smell of death and the ones who smell of life!" Alice Goodman, with her de Medici profile, in bold-print Marimekko dresses and big, translucent rings, glided around and made sure I fit into conversational groups. But she wasn't haughty—she was shy. I realized with a rush of surprise that I could see into her character, as if I were not a daughter-figure for her but a peer. We began to talk about the books we loved, about the strange doings of people, about the flashes of beauty in everyday life.

My mother ran into Alice Goodman in the market. "She adores you," she said to me with a trace of puzzlement. "Well, you know, I'm the ghost of their house past," I told her. But I was confused by the scorn with which I now eyed the unloved, unheeded (except by my father) pieces of respectable furniture in our living room. Surely my mother wasn't jealous of the Goodmans. She didn't have corrosive feelings like that.

Besides, she and I were never more companionable or twin-like than that summer, now that I was finally grown up and we were each behaving in a manner that was shocking to the milieu we'd both come from. It was that milieu's very narrowness that made us think ourselves identical. I got as big a lump in my throat as my mother did when the subject of Negro injustice came up. Part of my summer was spent, at her urging, at a Head Start preschool, reading to tiny, serious black children. It was exhilarating to be a saint, even twice a week. As for my music, my mother would slip into my room and stand there beaming as I practiced the violin. Even when I stormed out of a family orchestra rehearsal protesting, "I won't play with these amateurs"—my brothers and sisters—she only smiled, because she secretly thought arrogance was a necessary phase of my becoming a bolder version of her.

Anyway, how could she object to arrogance within the family when she kept leaving for meetings in the middle of dinner? In fact, my mother had worked out a new familial vision that not only contained but thrived on the eccentricity of its members. That vision was captured in the Christmas photo of 1965, for which we all posed right before I left for college. On her instructions, we put on clothes that "expressed our innermost selves," and we convened outside at the circular stone bench. The picture shows us grouped on that bench, smiling brightly, backed by the huge old trees of our yard—a cartoon collection of the dangerous urges that were just then sprouting in the bosom of the American family: urges for solitude, for oblivion, for magical domination.

On the far left I stand barefoot in my madras shift with long hair falling over one eye, playing my violin. I was eighteen. My sixteen-year-old brother Judd sits next to me in his mountain-climbing clothes; ten-year-old Mardy is a princess with a head-scarf for a crown; four-year-old Sam sports a Superman cape (no, Super*kitty*); seven-year-old Faith, home for the weekend, is in a dress and holding a rattle; my father is in full hunting regalia with his new dog, a pointer, sitting between his legs; my mother displays a "We Shall Overcome" button on her shirtwaist. The only strange note is struck by twelve-year-old Harry on the far right, who wears a button-down shirt and holds a bag of golf clubs. Harry was the reverse rebel: he was trying to be "normal."

A week later my mother drove me to college. We left at mid-day so as to push straight through the night, the way we drove to New Hampshire. For a while we sang songs together. Then we spelled each other at the wheel, one driving while the other slept. Toward evening we were both awake, somewhere in Indiana, and my mother grew thoughtful and anxious. She was driving. "The family, you know," she said, her eyes on the turnpike ahead, "is the best social unit yet devised by man—not perfect, but the best yet." Then it all came out in a rush, the flood of anxious thoughts. My generation was "exploring" sexual matters much more than hers had. But danger threatened. "You have to believe me," she pleaded. "Sexual adjustment with your partner takes months, even years. If you 'jump the gun,' you'll turn out less sensitive, hardened somehow."

"Oh, Mom, do we have to talk about this again?" I said; then, seeing her stricken face, I promised to think hard before I jumped the gun.

Silence fell. I looked out the window at the twilit fields flashing by on the edge of the turnpike. In local politics my mother was a hero. But in this deepest, most private way of being—in matters of love—she was a coward, and she was trying, I dimly felt, to blackmail me. She was saying that if I took a wrong turn, my character, my whole future, would be ruined. Of course I was scared of sex, terrified of getting pregnant—the mess, the ignominy—alarmed at the dark pull of excitement that seemed to belong to even the first stages of love, a pull that might suck you in until you'd changed your essential nature. All I'd done so far was tempt Gary in a motel room. Then I'd allowed, on some dates, a hand crawling up my thigh, a stupendous sensation. I'd also French-kissed a certain college-age neighbor in his house when his parents were away; and I'd lain with Ned Scharf on a blanket at night in our yard, while he reached inside my dress and felt my small breast. What such acts awoke in the flesh was powerful: they made my body feel like a new thing. I couldn't renounce that.

And we weren't talking just about sex. We were talking about all the sensations that I'd hoarded along the way, growing up beside my mother: extreme responses to ocean sky and dark golf courses, visceral reactions to poetry, now these new, confused feelings of pleasure at being touched by boys on dates. If I had a self of my own, separate from hers, it was composed of messages from my body that had kept me secret company for as long as I could remember, amusing, nourishing, telling me what was true. My mother didn't think the body could speak. I knew better.

We pulled up in the narrow street in front of Radcliffe's Cabot Hall at midafternoon the next day, exhausted and bedraggled in our madras skirts and loafers and pigtails. We'd both braided our hair in the night, to get it out of our eyes, in the ladies' room of some Pennsylvania rest stop. The Cabot Hall lobby was empty—we were early. But as we peered down the long halls, another mother and daughter came out of a room. The mother was tall, with a swirling red coat and a majestic hairdo. The daughter, in a navy blue coat, followed quietly behind. "How do you do," said the imposing mother, offering her hand, "I'm Flora Lewis, of *The New York Times*. I believe our daughters will be classmates . . ."

We all shook hands. My mother and I beamed modestly. We excused ourselves to find my room, on a higher floor. We lugged my trunk upstairs, and my beloved new stereo that looked like a white suitcase with speakers locked onto either end, and my violin in its case, which I cradled in my arms. "Be good, Fluff," said my mother. "I'm so excited for you." She went out quickly. I was left sitting on a hard chair, still holding my violin, staring at two thin, bare mattresses on the bunk beds in the little room, waiting for the unknown roommate. I trembled at my insubstantiality.

And my mother was out on the road alone. I put down the violin and went to the tall window that took up a whole wall of the room. The quadrangle of grass was darkening as day turned to evening. She was supposed to stay the night with friends in Dedham, Massachusetts, before she headed back across the country. As I learned later, she missed her Dedham exit off the Mass Pike. She went past it all the way to Framingham and had to retrace her route—she'd been crying too hard to see the road signs.

I HAD PINNED GREAT, CONFUSED, AND BARELY CON-
scious hopes on my new college. I had rejected Vassar without a
thought because it was just a girls' school; Radcliffe, being part of
imperious Harvard, meant the real world. And Harvard was my
father's, which suggested one last route to his worldly swagger, so
long off-limits to me because I was my mother's daughter. Radcliffe was also serving in my mind as the opposite: an antidote to
Harvard. Back home, even as I was deciding on my college
choice, my father was disabusing me in his usual flip style of the
hope of camaraderie with him. "Did you go to Radcliffe or did a
horse step on your face?" he used to say, chuckling, as he walked
through the kitchen. That was the favorite joke in *his* Harvard day.

"Stop it, you're horrible," I would say, but I would chuckle in
spite of myself. The more he insisted on his joke, though, the
more I harbored the furious thought that he was wrong; that

waiting for me at Radcliffe would be a kind of woman he didn't know about, who looked completely normal and could still match him in irony and charisma. When the freshman handbook had come in the mail that summer, I'd pored over the snapshots of my future classmates. Could this be the one, or this—who would lift me, by the alchemy of friendship, out of the circle of taunting and appeasement that enclosed the sexes in our house?

At the first "sherry" for freshmen in the old Cabot Hall living room, I pounced on these classmates, reciting their middle names and addresses, which I had involuntarily memorized. I was a whirlwind of personableness, to which the New York girls responded languidly. We all watched *Adam's Rib,* the old Hollywood movie from the year we were two (1949), starring Katharine Hepburn and Spencer Tracy as married lawyers. My euphoria peaked. "Can you believe they put women lawyers in the movies in those days?!" I said to the girl next to me as we rose, blinking, from our folding chairs.

Hepburn's patrician girlishness with Tracy reminded me of my mother, yet the character she played wore fitted business suits and high heels and had her own office and secretary. I didn't even notice that the movie also humiliated Hepburn, in the breakfast-making scene, for instance, where she gets everything wrong; the atmosphere of 1965 was still skewed to such humiliations. What ignited me was a historical conjunction, dimly perceived. Here was a picture of my mother's imaginary other life, the professional life she never had. It had jumped over time, in these flickering movie images, and landed on me. I could start up where Hepburn and my mother had left off.

But my mood deflated as the upperclassmen arrived and the academic year started. Mornings before classes, girls in my dorm rushed up and down the halls, grabbing clean clothes from the drying room near the stairwell; tugging down girdles under skirts; straightening stockings; smoothing hair in the mirrors of the communal bathrooms; securing little purses over shoulders. There was a mindless anxiety about these motions. Evenings, the preparations were more intense: powder was applied and fresh lipstick and perfume.

Clothes and makeup were what one needed to study at Widener Library, that massive redbrick structure at the bottom of Harvard Yard. A special cachet was attached to studying at night in the great reading room with the turquoise arched ceiling and the murals, on both sides of the stairs, of the females Victory and Death smothering some poor little soldier from World War I. You might meet somebody there, or on the way. Harvard Yard wasn't just the place where our lectures and classes happened and the library stayed open late, it was also an immense erotic zone for which you had to dress up. Inside those ancient brick walls, on the village-common paths among the upright old New England buildings, strolled men of all ages, in tweed and leather and zip-up jackets, conversing with high seriousness. There were so many of them compared to us—Radcliffe girls made up a tenth of undergraduates—that the Yard turned into a Cinderella's ball where, night or day, you might catch the eye of an upperclassman, a grad student, an assistant professor, and thus be inducted into the real life of the place.

My own ambitions receded; I focused instead on that tingling sensation of being watched, maybe chosen, as I rode my bike the half mile from the Radcliffe dorms to Harvard Yard, as I edged into a seat in lecture halls, or studied in Widener in the evening. It was like going out on a hunt—as the prey. All this was made bearable by my roommate, Ellen Mandel, who came with some worldly resources she was willing to share. We had found each other in the dorm lunchroom during a conversation in which it was revealed that she spoke French as prodigiously as I. This sudden checkmate to each other's superiority shocked us into switching roommates in order to room together. Ellen came from Scarsdale. Over a New York weekend she and her sad-eyed, fur-coated mother took me to a cluttered store in the old Jewish immigrant part of Manhattan, Orchard Street, where, under a disheveled pile of clothes, lay a blue-and-white-checked mock Chanel suit "slashed to nothing."

That suit transformed me: its little nipped waist canceled the haphazard midwesternness of the rest of my wardrobe. It brought me glances in Widener, trysts in coffee shops, tickets to football games, even a lovesick admirer, Gregory. But these encounters occurred in a mental fog so deep that the cavaliers are unrecallable. I can see the pink shaved neck of an upperclassman at a football game and taste the smooth-burning Brandy Alexander he had brought in a silver flask. I can see someone else's bow tie reflected in the blue neon sign of the hip Blue Parrot coffee shop. I can remember the whole of Gregory, a whimsical blond youth in a tight tweed suit and an ascot, because he scared me. Or rather, my own dullness about him scared me. He'd grown up in India. He was exotic. He was on fire about me. I felt nothing for him.

My inner self drew back from registering what young men might mean to me because of a sensation, tugging away inside, that something even more fundamental hadn't been settled. I didn't yet have a female self, or rather, I couldn't get to it here at Radcliffe, under the layers of hurt and anxiety and bravado that had accumulated from life at home. Ellen had also brought a primal edginess from her home. She and I were opposites on the outside: she was Jewish, as she compulsively reminded me. She had a comically suave walk, like Groucho Marx, and a raucous self-derision that caused her to say in the face of compliments, "I wouldn't want to be a member of any club that let *me* in." But our longing to be what Harvard wanted us to be fused us uneasily together.

Surely there existed some facet of ourselves that could be redone so that everything would fall into place. Maybe it was weight: we ate only lettuce and cottage cheese for dinner. Maybe it was perfume: we debated the different scents. And we practiced dressage on our very personalities. "Resolved: I must be proud in movement and mind," I wrote in the gray cloth journal that went everywhere with me; also, "I must be a little less careful and a little more colorful."

I was terrified of falling into my mother's earnest mode, but earnestness, helpfulness, and intense displays of empathy welled up whenever I was unsure. "Charity—listening to people—eases a little that knot concerning their not liking me," I told my journal on one melancholy day. In that first semester of college, the tension between an unwanted nostalgia for home and an unrealizable need to impress in my new environment caused my natural buoyancy to drain away, along with what had passed for hope. I stopped practicing the violin. Cabot Hall had assigned me a storage room downstairs to practice in, with a sagging armchair where the ladies of the kitchen sometimes flopped down for a smoke, even when I was playing.

My unconscious despair didn't come just from my own haunted social ambitions. It came from Radcliffe's role inside Harvard, which, despite all protestations to the contrary, was that of abject supplicant. Founded in Harvard's shadow in 1879 as an "annex" where girls could hear lectures from Harvard professors without credit, Radcliffe had been inching since its beginning toward a merger that Harvard didn't seem to want at all. Over the years, events had shoved the women partway inside: in 1943, when war removed the men, Radcliffe girls went into Harvard classes "temporarily." In 1963, after twenty years of Harvard classes, Radcliffe graduates finally began to receive Harvard diplomas. In 1965 we Radcliffe freshmen were so eager to belong that we were blind to the signs of inequality: our cramped double rooms (Harvard students had suites), the total absence of female professors. One sole tenured female professor taught at Harvard then, in mathematics. I never saw her. The category "female professor" was unimaginable to us undergraduates. In an academic mirror of the future, there were no reflections of us. Yet we were sure that Harvard was the noblest place on earth.

We were living in the last surviving moment of the Cold War–era arrangement of the genders. In just four years, out of small cells of Boston feminists called Bread and Roses, the concept of sisterhood would be born; Yale, then Princeton, would invite women into their gates as equals; even Harvard would start merger and cohabitation talks with Radcliffe. Stockings, girdles, high heels, bras—the infrastructure of femininity—would be cast aside, though skirts were required in Harvard classes as late as 1969. But none of this was foreseeable in 1965: the stylistic disparities dwelled so deep within us they couldn't be projected out; we couldn't look at Harvard and say what was wrong.

Within our own world of Radcliffe, though, we were stringent judges of the social scene. We nurtured a casual scorn of the rituals that seemed to persist from a musty feminine past: the conferences with those matter-of-fact, gray-haired Radcliffe deans; the compulsory sherries in our dorms; the sit-down dinners where we served one another; the freshman curfew of 9 P.M.; the Saturday night milk and cookies in the dorm living room for those who had no dates. I was among those who fought to retire the milk and cookies, but a faint terror shadowed my argument. What if some Saturday night I didn't have a date? I would need milk and cookies. And one of the class beauties, a diplomat's daughter with a closetful of formal gowns, put herself among the dateless misfits to back milk and cookies. Did she do it out of charity, or did she know something I didn't?

Sometimes, late at night in the common room on Cabot Hall's third floor, the utopian Radcliffe that I had once hoped to find appeared all on its own. Girls would drift in from studying, slump on chairs, and make remarks about books, the world, their parents. The air would be filled with ironic metaphors, choice adjectives, deadpan forays into precarious emotions . . . "When my stepmother calls," said my favorite senior, an heiress-waif from New York, "she inserts a stiletto thrust somewhere in the conversation. And you know those wounds from stilettos are more lethal than the ones from big knives." My blood raced. No one in St. Louis had admitted that family members used stilettos on one another.

At moments like these the room was stirred to solidarity. A density of intelligence and sympathy absorbed even idle remarks. A shameful happiness filled the air. But nothing held such moments in place; no permission from within allowed them to exist. All too soon would come a cold draft of envy, of posturing. On Cabot Hall's third floor, it came in the person of Jenette Kahn, a tall, slim-hipped, black-haired professor's daughter from Cincinnati. Jenette strolled languidly up and down the halls; she pouted; she tossed off faint bromides; and she trailed in her wake those demons of dismay, anxiety, and shame at the meager social skills the rest of us had brought from home. I have a vivid recollection of Jenette draped in the common room doorway, of our nervous shifts in our chairs in response to her posing, of her announcement in a kittenish voice that what she really needed now was "a *lime mousse*."

Jenette took my roommate, Ellen, under her wing and told her what to wear to Widener Library. But I spoiled my own potential for coaching with the questions that kept popping out of my mouth: "What's a lime mousse? What's a Bialystok bagel? What's *The New York Review of Books*?" Such brilliant new languages—the language of confession, the language of sophistication—flowed by me with their warm and cold currents, as currents drift by a tired swimmer. I had to learn them right then and put them to use. But the enormity of such a task pushed me toward escape, at least on the weekends. Nobody called it escaping. Everyone thought I was responsible and enterprising. I got a waitress job Fridays and Saturdays in a French restaurant called Maître Jacques, in Boston's Back Bay. I just walked in and they hired me for my French. Waitressing was supposed to keep that French alive and earn me the money to go to Germany that summer, to work in a hotel—Lufthansa Airlines was placing students in unskilled jobs—and jump-start my German. I was taking German to acquire a second foreign language so I could major in European History and Literature.

What the waitress job really offered was a way to check in with my old dreamy self, the old me who hadn't yet arrived at the radiant future but was happily suspended along the way. When I got off the subway Friday evenings on the gray bridge at Charles Street and walked alone through echoing old Beacon Hill to my restaurant, I could talk to myself again and mix myself up with imaginary people in the strange houses. And as I came near it, the yellow-lit restaurant below sidewalk level shone out like an airport in a strange land. I opened the door. *"Salut! Bienvenue! Comment va notre petite étudiante?"* ("How is our little student?") cried Odile, Francine, Lily, Marie-France, Chérie, the collection of middle-aged French souls who had washed up on the shores of New England. They were my other society, my antiworld. The kitchen sent its boeuf bourguignon smells wafting to the dining room; we put the red-checked tablecloths on the tables, and the knives and forks and stand-up napkin triangles. And when *les clients* arrived, we swung in and out of the kitchen hefting trays, winking at one another and exchanging French retorts—all the mothers and the one ecstatic daughter.

MEANWHILE, MY REAL mother hovered in my psyche like a faraway lover I couldn't bear to think about. She loomed larger as vacations approached, and I prepared to cross back from the restless Harvard present to the settled St. Louis past. She was always waiting at the airport with a face of bright expectancy. When I had returned to Harvard, a steady stream of letters came from home, which I read with eagerness mixed with weariness. "Sam has almost stopped wetting his bed"; "Mardy is working hard at her cello"; "Dad's new 'hawk house' is almost finished . . ." I wrote letters back over freshman year, practicing my powers of description, needing to hear my voice in the echo chamber of her mind, like a person rehearsing a speech in an empty auditorium.

Our correspondence peaked when I went to Germany the summer of 1966, after freshman year. I had been placed by Lufthansa in a hotel of rustic brick, in a tiny village on a little lake in Schleswig-Holstein, near the East German border. The hotel owners, a brassy middle-aged couple, hid a sadistic streak in their bustling persons. I was supposed to clean all twenty rooms *schnell schnell* (quickly quickly) in the morning, but I could never finish in time, so I was late and flustered in joining the team of old ladies who washed the mountains of noontime dishes in the kitchen. At 4 P.M. busloads of tourists came to our hotel for cake and coffee; cascades of dirty cake plates and coffee cups prolonged the work into the night.

Shocked by the loneliness of physical labor, I sent out an SOS for mail, and my mother responded valiantly every few days. The village postmistress, who worked in our kitchen, brought the letters in the morning. I kept them in my apron. I retreated after work to a cemetery on a hill across the street to read them while propped against a gravestone and eating a bag of cookies under the luminous clouds of twilight. At night, in my back room over the hotel garden, I wrote home, pouring out the frustration, the resentment, the homesickness I knew would find a quick echo in my mother's justice-hungry heart. "Frau Wegen has said not one good thing about my work but today at 2 she started yelling at me for various small things, and I was fighting tears, and two of the old ladies who work with me in the kitchen (East German refugees) noticed and told me everything which lifted the veil on this place—namely, that Frau Wegen seems to be a devil; it all depends on how she sleeps the night before or how much she has drunk. . . ."

My isolation, though, brought a strange calm. One day the

thought struck, as I leaned on my broom in a sun-filled guest room, that I was my own companion. There was defiance involved, since the brooms and mops I carried between hotel and annex marked me as the unprivileged. *"Bist du Spanischerin? Bist du Turkin?"* the village kids asked ("Are you Spanish? Are you a Turk?"). What a novelty, to be taken for a third-world "guest worker." A faint reverence for America, where anyone could be anything, began to bloom, linked to the homey bottle of Jim Beam I'd bought for my coworkers on the Fourth of July, which stood half full on the bureau all summer.

One early morning in the hotel kitchen, my defiance congealed in a resolve to abandon the study of this alien Europe. Or else it was a revulsion to the tureen of cold goose fat and bread that was our breakfast that day. In my room upstairs I'd gotten to the part of Faulkner's *Intruder in the Dust* when the garrulous young narrator is fed hot eggs and biscuits at 3 A.M. by the sheriff. That phantom Faulknerian breakfast pushed me out of my European reverie into a free fall toward home. My waif-heiress friend had been telling me all year to forget Europe and study American history and literature. "It's like psychology—you find out who you are." I came back to Harvard and poured out my breakfast story; a dubious dean agreed to the switch.

A PROUD AND edgy band of seven—four women and three men—convened for our first seminar in what was then an exclusive major. We were a typical array of provincial "best students" in that last moment before the hippie movement: a gamin, a deep-ponderer, two faux skeptics, two aesthetes, and I, the last one in, jumping out of my skin with friendliness. Our topic was *Redburn,*

Herman Melville's little-known 1849 novel about his first sea voyage, when he was a wellborn but impoverished youth trying to be a common sailor. Poor Redburn had some trouble with snobbery. He'd outfitted himself with a red flannel shirt and a gentleman's fowling piece; he had no sailor's skills; nobody helped him; he tried courtesy toward his shipmates, and they mocked him. Suddenly, in one of those flashes that education is supposed to produce, Redburn was me. His beloved, shabby New York home merged in my mind with our falling-down mansion in St. Louis, and with the figure of my father stalking around a corner toward the backyard. I saw suddenly that America had always meant this: the endless negotiations inside oneself between privilege and abjectness; the endless climbing up and sliding down of slippery social cliffs. I squirmed joyously in my chair. The professor paused and asked me what was wrong. I replied in confusion that I was having an epiphany, that I myself was "decayed gentility."

"So delighted you are loving your studies," wrote my mother that fall, then added a little plaintively, "Why don't you start jotting post-cards home? What aspects of Amer. History are you into?" I had stopped writing home because of a sudden impulse to protect my new territory. Guilt stabbed me as I looked up from her letter. She wouldn't understand. She'd never thought about the confusion lurking in the very ideas of class and snobbery. Class for her was something you had to work to erase; snobbery was simply a sin. But I'd been handed a way to bypass the moral view: to look at the past not for signs of progress, but for the spectacle of everything mixed together—virtue and vice, pride and shame, nobility and greed. I'd been handed a way to look at her world on my terms.

We were doing the era of Andrew Jackson (1829–37), when

the "little man" of farms and cities first challenged the eastern gentry. That was just before the historian William H. Prescott wrote his pioneering book about sixteenth-century Peru, *The History of the Conquest of Peru*—a book in which "speculators and adventurers swarmed like so many famished harpies, in the track of discovery." He was really writing it, though, about the Jacksonian horde of rough-and-tumble citizens in his own time who threatened what was fine-textured in the national psyche. Oh, the layers of history. Over and over, the rabble had routed the aesthetes. I'd been boxed into a view at home of people getting better all the time. But people were awful: even in our time, harpies and adventurers in our government were swarming all over Vietnam.

That fall Robert McNamara, the secretary of defense, came to Harvard to give a speech. Antiwar students surrounded his car, immobilized it, rocked it, and imprisoned him in it for several hours as a protest against that runaway war. Bobby Post, my American History and Lit brother, lay down in front of the car. That jolted us into real alarm. He could be expelled. He could be drafted and sent to Vietnam. But instead of jumping into the antiwar movement, like fellow classmates, I got sidetracked by the sudden discovery of another dispossessed population in American history, more problematic even than faded gentility: the women. Women, it turned out, were a persistent conundrum of our country's past.

Halfway through the second volume of the eerily penetrating 1835 book *Democracy in America,* by the French nobleman Alexis de Tocqueville, two short chapters sent chills up my spine—"Education of Girls in the United States" and "The Young Woman as Wife." Girls were given more freedom here, observed Tocqueville, than anywhere else he knew, and they were trusted; they were urged to have opinions. But those same girls, when they married, gave up all that freedom and became willing prisoners of their own homes. It was still that way. How could Tocqueville have known, over a century earlier, what it would be like in St. Louis in the 1960s? How had he divined these two types: me with my surfeit of freedom, and my mother in her anxious bondage? Tocqueville wasn't the only one who saw the paradox. Hawthorne, Crane, James, Wharton—all the classic authors in our American Lit survey—wrote books about that new-style heroine our country had added to the world's collection of archetypes: the proud, uncertain, brave yet tragic American girl, awash in a sea of independence.

"I've got your number," said my tutor, Marshall Cohen, who was big and bearlike and said "Take care" at the end of tutorial, which almost made me cry, to hear a *man* say that. "You just slot your 'American girl' into whatever course you're taking and write a paper on her. But do try to temper the enthusiasm." He was right on both counts. I had found a home within academia, and excitement bred hyperbole. Then, as school rolled on through colonial history, Gilded Age history, literature, and poetry, another, smaller female population caught my attention: not the mass of girls, but the women—just a few—who had declined to pass from girlhood to wifehood; who had become writers instead of wives.

Against Tocqueville's backdrop of ubiquitous female conformity, these single souls stood out in wondrous nakedness. Margaret Fuller, the New England intellectual mocked by her male compatriots, went to Italy and found a hero (Garibaldi), a younger lover, and a better prose style. Sarah Orne Jewett lived alone in her native Maine and wrote stories about the folk wisdom of older women. Emily Dickinson spent her life in her father's house in Amherst, nurturing an inner hurricane of sensations and metaphors.

> *The soul selects her own society,*
> *Then shuts the door;*
> *On her divine majority*
> *Obtrude no more.*

How imperious! How unanxious! These were the women I had come to Radcliffe to find. Maybe they were dead, but I could adopt them anyway.

This awe at women writers explains a friendship that almost drowned me in my middle years at college. Robin Von Breton, of my History and Lit band, had white-blond, curly hair, little round glasses, and a face screwed up in mock apology. "I'm faded gentility too," she'd whispered to me after the *Redburn* seminar. But she was also a poet, really a poet. She had gotten into Robert Lowell's seminar. She had taken the last year off to work; she was a year older. And she connected, in her person, Harvard intellect with an enlightened female sensuality I'd only dreamt about—or rather, it was enlightened connoisseurship, that future province of our generation.

What a self-dramatizing and needy soul Robin must have been then, though I couldn't see it. She had worked for the architects Charles and Ray Eames. She wore a sky-blue coat with a black velvet collar, and a straw hat. She took notes in turquoise ink. She typed her poems with a blue typewriter ribbon on crinkly onionskin. She brought me to a shop on Brattle Street with tall glass windows, Design Research, where they had Marimekko smock dresses from Finland in wild-colored amoeba prints—the only clothes worth wearing. Robin seemed to swoop around Cambridge like a person in a Chagall painting. I followed after like a midwestern Sancho Panza, administering reassurance and bright ideas. Robin kept saying how much she needed me, how I was steady, warm, and comforting.

But Robin drifted away in the middle of the year because of Denny, a blond poet from Dartmouth with a motorcycle, big boots, and an embarrassed grin. She drove north to visit him in the middle of the night, or he came roaring down to her. Poets were supposed to be in love, she said. So I plunged back into the social whirl and found Noel, a tall sophomore from Florida with wavy black hair and a ruddy child's face. We looked splendid together, said Robin.

In a halfhearted encounter in Noel's Harvard room, with the door open a crack to the outside world, he and I fumbled toward sexual knowledge. Virginity was crossed off the list. But our shame at feeling nothing pushed us apart. I fixed my sights next on one of our demigods, Cruce Stark, a History and Lit grad student from East Texas with a southern twang and a boyish grin. I won him in the library with the help of a very short polka-dotted dress. Sex took on the coloring of his shabby boardinghouse room. I lost him at a party. After a lot of whiskey he confessed that he was in love with someone else. We careered in his car over icy streets—I thought we would crash. I forgave him, as my mother had taught me, and we went on, benumbed.

He wasn't the only one. At Harvard in 1966, a round of meetings and partings took place. If a current flowed between you and someone, you went home with him. Bedsheets and warm bodies paraded through my life. Thin, sensitive men gave way to big, pinkish men; foreigners followed southerners. My mother had no clear idea that the maternal scaffolding she'd raised around my purity had simply dropped away. She would ask in letters if I had a current "beau"; I snorted at the term. I was becoming a seasoned sexual being, if statistics were the measure. By the spring of junior year I listed ten "slept-withs" in my journal: Noel, Benito, Johnny, Irving, Harvey, Peter, Pete, Cruce, Bruce, Scott—though four, I noted, had been mistakes.

I didn't know then that I was avoiding all emotions and sleep-walking through sex like a robot or a call girl. Through an unconscious effort of will I kept it casual, like dessert at the end of a meal. You could do that then, because sex wasn't sex; it was just one of the signs of personal triumph over the inhibitions that had been so mistakenly foisted on us in the tight little world of home.

In Cambridge, Massachusetts, in the late sixties, doubts about sex were swallowed up in the general euphoria of a new order. Everything had loosened up—not just sex. Dresses were unfitted and just hung. Without a girdle, one's pelvis was fleshy. Talk tumbled over itself; pauses could be used in place of words; riding a bike felt like swimming through the air. Strangers smiled at each other. *"C'est tellement simple, l'amour,"* said the mysterious Garence (always backlit) in *Les Enfants du Paradis,* which played perpetually at the Brattle Cinema. It was the movie of our generation, made presciently in Paris in 1945. "You make me feel like a na-tur-al wo-man," sang Aretha Franklin on the record player in Ellen's and my room. That was our song; "natural" was our word. Marijuana was our drug. Ellen had tried this pungent stuff in Europe the summer after freshman year and brought some back. You smoked it in a fat cigarette; you held the smoke in till your throat ached, and then you felt the world waver, open, and spill into your senses.

Maybe, we said after a few inhalations, we'd been imprinted at birth with a primal delight—our parents' primal delight, since they had wanted us so much, after the war. Wasn't it our duty to revive that delight, since they had misplaced it, somewhere along the way?

REAL LIFE NOW resided at college. Home life, when I went back for vacations, was a spectacle to which I lent my polite attention. I listened graciously to brothers and sisters explaining how they'd mastered a two-wheeler, or sneaked into my bathroom and examined my lipsticks, or learned to set off fireworks without burning their fingers. I heard with detached interest my mother's descriptions of her newest black friends, of the cross-race dialogue group she'd started at church, of her letter to the Veiled Prophet Ball board proposing incorporation of black debutantes into the city's holiest of social rites. That was bold, I said, throwing her a compliment from the lofty heights of my new world.

Then I retreated to my room to study, or took the car to the Goodmans' to talk about art, or drove around the city and had sex with a misplaced Danish Mexican whom I'd met at a party. If it was spring vacation, I disappeared for hours into the backyard to sunbathe. Half my dorm had gone off to Florida; I didn't have the money. But St. Louis was the South, from a Boston perspective. At least it was warmer than Boston, where the trees were still bare and the wind harsh. I would take a lounge chair and a blanket outside to lie shivering for hours in the pale spring sun. This was a provocative activity, since my father was the one who had been crazy about the sun. Now I had his sun fetish, which my mother couldn't understand. "You're going out there again? But it's so cold!" "The life of the senses," I would remind her.

My father had consolidated his own life of the senses in a curious way. He'd fallen obsessively into the business of breeding falcons, which I observed rather vaguely when I went home. One of his prairie falcons, Taka, laid eggs sometime in early 1967. Two were fertile. A young couple named Charlie and Gerry Brewer came to help care for the falcons. They lived in the maids' rooms above the kitchen. Taka's eggs hatched at the end of May, the end of my sophomore year; one chick, Arthur, named for my Kendall grandfather, lived for six days. Falcons had never bred in captivity, except once in Germany before the war. The next spring, another lot of Taka's eggs hatched. Three chicks lived. Falconers around the country were watching the proceedings. My father became famous to readers of that modest national publication *Hawk Chalk*. He rushed home from work, said my mother, to peer through the one-way glass window he'd installed in the hawk house and see who was breeding, who was nesting, who was growing.

But all this hubbub and my father's expanded team of falconer-disciples upset the age-old family alignment. My brothers couldn't help but be drawn into the near hysteria about the hawks and falcons. As a result, my mother's once-loyal army of children was sadly depleted. Alone with her reform work, she must have longed for me to slip back, on vacations, to my post as her lieutenant. Suffused with the superiority of college life, I proved less than loyal.

Things came to a head between the two of us over Christmas vacation of junior year. It was my second-to-last day home. The presents and church services and grandparents' dinners had come and gone; so had my mother's favorite moment in the year—caroling on Christmas Eve in the bitter cold, with her children singing around her. That morning she passed my room as I was coming out. "I hope you're still planning to visit Aunt Junie in the nursing home," she said. My great-great-aunt was still alive, though she'd been moved from the hotel where she had long held coquettish court, to the stark atmosphere of a semi-hospital. "Why?" I said. "I have to study."

My mother blinked in surprise. "How long can it take to drive downtown and see an old lady?" she asked quietly.

"It doesn't matter to Aunt Junie if I visit her," I retorted. "She won't know me. Last Christmas she didn't even put the ten dollars in our gift envelopes—they were empty, remember?"

"You have to go see her," said my mother, "your grandmother would be hurt."

"I won't," I said, and I felt that flick of an inner switch pouring a current into my perverse resolve. Tears of disbelief welled in my mother's eyes. I stood my ground as a cacophony of thoughts invaded my head, edged with a shadow of fear: *I don't have to do this; I don't have to take care of everybody; I don't have to be good; I have my own life.* Our drive to the airport the next day was silent. My mother let me out of the car and I hauled out my bags; we barely said good-bye.

This was my one and only rebellious act against my mother, which I'd been trying to formulate since my early teens. Rebellion had been a near impossibility with her politics. She was on the right side of everything: retarded children, civil rights, Vietnam (she had followed Martin Luther King Jr.'s lead on that). It was the infernal scent of goodness that pushed me over the edge.

I had to be negligent just once. I rebelled against goodness. Then she rebelled at my rebellion. "At first I thought, while you were still home," she wrote in a letter that followed me to college, "that I would maybe never again have quite the same respect for you that I have had for so long, on account of what I consider a mistake in your instincts (the nursing home incident)." The words fell like stones on my heart. She talked about some nameless acts in her own past that would always make her "a tiny bit ashamed," and of the generous people who had forgiven *her*—as if I should be grateful for her forgiveness. It didn't feel like forgiveness. Forgiveness—*she* thought it solved everything.

The letter waxed hot and cold, now blaming me, now blaming herself for what she'd made of me. "It is possible that in my pride and in my joy at discovering you as a person whose ideas I could respect," she wrote, "it is *possible* that I have contributed to a tendency toward self-centered behavior on your part." She said she would try to lay out my duties more clearly when I was home, and recognize my needs and wants as being "completely different" from hers. But she ended on the attack: "I'm sure all this would sound more intelligent if couched in professional jargon—to which you are more accustomed. I just hope it will communicate 'love' to you . . ."

Here was a punitive mother I'd never encountered, but one who sounded lonely and abandoned too. What had I done that was so terrible? I read and reread the letter in the too-bright winter sun in my room. I'd paraded all my blithe feelings of superiority in front of her. "She's found me out," I thought. "She knows I'm selfish to the core." I went next door to see if Ellen was there—her room was empty. I went up and down the hall, looking for Jamie or Ronnie, someone in my group. I wanted to talk about the stuff of our lives—exams, classes, clothes, anything to ground me in college again. The dorm was empty.

Maybe my mother's tone had something to do with the previous summer, when she had finally incurred the wrath of her oldest friends. She had taken some little kids and their friends to swim at the country club, forgetting, or so she said, that one five-year-old boy was black. After an eerie silence at the pool, the phone rang off the hook at home. "We support your community work, Betty, but for Chrissake leave us our private club!" My mother had examined the club bylaws, rejected the unwritten ones, called up liberal members, and told them to bring a black guest. She did everything right and she won that fight. But she had been hurt by those so-called friends, and maybe she had turned her new, bleak vision onto her daughter—once her double—and found even me a hypocrite.

Time passed. Letters went back and forth between us with apologies and explanations. The surface was patched up. In April we sobbed together on the phone when Martin Luther King Jr. was killed. She told me about a benefit she was hosting for Freedom of Residence. FOR had a case going to the Supreme Court, *Jones* v. *Mayer,* about a mixed-race couple who had been denied a house in the St. Louis suburb of Paddock Woods. To raise money they had imported a play from the East, *In White America.* "I wish you could meet these interracial actors," my mother said on the phone, "they're fascinating people."

Underneath, disquiet simmered. My mother wasn't proud of me anymore. My life was galloping off into the night to places unknown. So I folded in on myself to protect the indigestible fact of my selfishness, like an oyster closing in on a pearl.

· · ·

SCHOOL GREW MORE intense. History and Lit required a senior thesis. Mine would be about women authors, though I didn't
know which ones. But I had a graduate student named Ann Douglas as a thesis adviser. I'd been scared of her. She was the consum-
mate Harvard legend: lean, tan, blond, longhaired—yet she'd
finished Radcliffe summa cum laude, she was doing a dual Ph.D.
in American and medieval studies, she had a nice graduate-
student husband. We had met my sophomore year in the faculty
club, where I was a waitress and she was a diner. She had taken a
liking to me; I couldn't understand why.

But when we started our tutorial in the fall of 1968, all the
cautiousness of Harvard hierarchies fell away in a blaze of discovery. It was the cusp of a new time. Ann had been pulled into a
local cell of Bread and Roses, which had let loose a conspiratorial
girlishness in her that took the strain off me. "Read this—Margaret Fuller learned to be simple in Italy," I would say, bursting
into Ann's living room at Eliot House, or "Edith Wharton *had* to
put a man at the center of this novel—she couldn't imagine a
woman ambitious enough." I have a vivid memory of the greenish
rug, of medieval-looking chairs with green velvet cushions, of the
round wooden table where I spread my books and notes—and
Ann and me, almost standing in our excitement, on either side of
the table. One day I brought in an old library copy of Harriet
Beecher Stowe's 1870 novel, *Pink and White Tyranny*. "Don't mind
the title, it's about the cult of adornment," I said. "I'm in the subway," she shouted over the phone two days later. "You're right
about *Pink and White Tyranny*. This is the really important book."

Suddenly my old dreamy self had company. Ann was there, saying I was smart. My brother Judd was a Harvard freshman. He'd been to school in England and come back with long hair and a bandanna around his head; his presence lent a physical volume to the part of me that came from the family. I shared an apartment off campus with Robin, though that arrangement went bad. I'd picked an under-the-eaves third floor of a Cambridge apartment for its bohemian aura; she didn't like it. Anyway, Jack Davis from History and Lit moved into the apartment with us and she married him in December, which left me homeless.

I was offered instead, by a vote of my former Cabot Hall mates, their fourth-floor common room. That's where I went to live, under a concave bay window with no curtains—alone, but in the center of a crystal of well-wishers who wanted me back. I remember the dawns, appearing above me in every pane of the window. They woke me to excitement because of the thesis I was writing about the women writers I'd finally picked: Fuller, Stowe, and Kate Chopin, who had each described, in a different era, the dead-end state of becoming a wife. I called it "The Secret Springs of Revolution." Writing it was the first sustained work I'd ever done. The happiness of that work got mixed up with those blush-colored mornings in the bay window and the dark nights in Radcliffe's new curtainless library across the Quad.

As I was finding my bearings in a life of the mind, my mother was realizing herself in a life of action. In June 1968 St. Louis Freedom of Residence had hit the limelight when *Jones* v. *Mayer* triumphed in the Supreme Court. It was a great victory for a tiny ad hoc organization. A young St. Louis lawyer had argued the case in the highest court with funds raised by FOR. Discrimination in private subdivisions all across the country was officially illegal. My mother was jubilant and amazed.

I barely registered this milestone victory because she barely mentioned it in her letters. It seemed she was keeping her near-professional role in fair housing in a compartment separate from the family. But, as I found out later from the papers left after her death, the taste of victory only deepened my mother's resolve to go on. She was FOR's main fund-raiser. "New discriminatory maneuvering," as she put it, had sprouted among real estate agents after the victory. "Now that we have the legal tool to proceed," she wrote the Danforth Foundation in the fall of 1968, "can you see the critical importance of prompt and widespread filing of federal suits? The forces which will be seeking to subvert the law *must* be shown that there will be consequences. . . ."

My mother took up yet another kind of action in 1968, speaking on the Panel of American Women. This she mentioned glancingly in letters to me; I knew she had joined, but I thought the panel kind of homey. The St. Louis panel, a spin-off of the original panel in Kansas City started by the dynamic Ruth Brown— the child in the 1954 *Brown* v. *Board of Education*—had thirty-odd members. Five at a time, a Catholic, a black, a Jew, a white Anglo-Saxon Protestant, and a moderator, went out to church groups, womens' groups, school groups, clubs, and civic organizations all over Missouri to speak about themselves and their hopes for a better society.

Speaking on that panel made my mother what she'd always wanted to be: a performer, an orator, almost a minister. Panelists remember her leaning forward in incandescent earnestness, recounting her parents' civic efforts and her agonized realization that these weren't enough. The Protestant's panel role was the hardest, everyone said: how to explain a life of privilege. At the end of her talk, my mother pulled out the stops and told of the awful moment in 1946, at Vassar, when she'd arranged some "coon songs" handed down from her southern grandmother for her singing group, and mortally offended a black classmate. "I was almost literally on my knees in the next few days," went the speech's climax, "often in tears, begging forgiveness from her, begging her to believe that we had been thoughtless and stupid, but not purposefully rude . . ." Then she sent out her punch-line thought, that WASPs today must start seeing the things "that should have been as plain as the nose on the front of our faces . . ."

Even if I was inattentive to her personal triumphs, my mother couldn't help sharing one in November 1968. She got a job. It was tremendous news. I hadn't even known she wanted one, though if I had thought about the two tuitions at Harvard, I could have seen the need for it. Those job-hunting letters, which I found much later, reveal how much she agonized over this last step toward her own independence: credibility in the job market. They are at once too confident and too humble. She wrote most of them to TV stations, evoking the agitated state of St. Louis politics, the racial violence in other cities, the recent findings of the President's Riot Commission—and proposing herself as the host of a series of cross-race dialogues. "I rather think I have enough of the 'ham' in me to do this," she wrote to the TV executives, "after learning the *business* from you."

It wasn't a TV station that hired her in the end, but the Danforth Foundation, who knew her from FOR. They asked her to do a survey of preschool education in St. Louis. "I have a temporary, part-time bit of work to do for the Foundation," was what she wrote me almost timidly in late 1968. We saw its scale when we went home that Christmas. Index cards, charts, books, and piles of paper were spread out on the dining room table and on nearby chairs. The room looked like my college room in the throes of my thesis.

"How can you work so near the front door?" I asked her. "Doesn't everybody interrupt you?"

"I like it at the center of the house," she said.

By March 1969 she was done with the survey. She had earned her first paycheck of her life, $850. She was giddy with accomplishment. She had an idea how to spend it and make us a family again. "You and Judd have spring vacation the week before Easter," said a postcard in March. "Harry, Mardy and Sam have theirs the week *after* Easter." The postcard proposed that the family drive down to the Gulf coast of Alabama—"*all* of us, and then you and Judd could have the weekend on the beach, and fly back to Cambridge from there. What do you think? Love, Mom."

I read it as a gift to me—as the start of what could have been a whole new era in both our lives. She had earned her first money on her own; now she could acknowledge my sun fetish, my finished thesis, my imminent graduation. We could banish forever that terrible moment when I'd refused to visit Aunt Junie, who had since died and posthumously dashed everyone's hopes with the meagerness of her estate. "How did you know I've been dreaming of the ocean?" I wrote back. But it was also my mother's gesture to herself, I thought belatedly. She had finished a job too. She had earned some pleasure.

Pleasure was already seeping into her life, or at least a new tolerance for it. Over Christmas she'd sent me to her gynecologist to be fitted for a diaphragm, although I had one, unknown to her. "You're kidding," I'd said when she proposed this. "I have to go with the times," she answered, "though I'll never think it's right." She came out of the movie *Yellow Submarine* with my brother Judd and remarked that "we're raising a generation of poets." She had invited Greig Veeder, an old playmate of Judd's from Wickersham Lane, to live with us. He was twenty, a cocky kid with a prissy mother. He'd been arrested for marijuana possession, my mother told me on the phone just before spring vacation. He refused to live at home while he was waiting to go to a fancy psychological clinic.

"Bravo, you're making a commune," I said on the phone. The old house did look scruffily communal as Judd and I drove up in a cab after flying home on student standby. The spring grass was overgrown. The door was standing open. My mother answered our shout from the kitchen. We dropped our suitcases and went in to her. Our old playmate Greig was there, leaning against the wall with his hands in his pockets. For a minute I didn't want a commune. Then Sam, aged seven, rushed in and was tackled by Judd. Harry and Mardy, a leggy fourteen and fifteen, came home from school, threw down their schoolbooks, and joined the clump. Harry bowed. "Welcome, older siblings," he said. Mardy was going to be pretty. She was showing promise on the cello, said my mother. My father arrived at dusk and offered a dry cheek and a pat on the back before he changed into his hunting clothes and went out to his birds.

In the midst of the shifting throng my mother looked as young and bright as anyone. She wore an old flannel shirt and a wraparound skirt. Her skin was soft, unmarked by makeup except the basic red lipstick she always wore, and the glasses magnifying her eyes. I was older now than she was when she married and had me. Why did I succumb to a subtle unease about my own person when I was with her? I'd put on rings and perfume and a silk scarf for the plane trip. Now I felt as I always felt lately with her: wrong, artificial—and superior and tender and so torn in my heart.

"I dressed up to come home," I explained, "practice for jobhunting."

"You look wonderful," she said.

I DID GET a job during that spring vacation. It wasn't what she'd had in mind for me. She had been sending me St. Louis addresses of settlement houses, inner-city churches, newspapers. It was only a halfhearted attempt; she knew I wouldn't come home after college. "I thought of a profession for us both," she'd even written. "We can start a dialogue across the generations. We could take it national." I smiled sadly at that one. But I also had my own ideas about jobs, and I'd sent my letters out to travel magazines and travel agencies. A St. Louis–based agency called Open Road had written back and asked me for an interview. I drove downtown in my blue-and-white suit and parried worldly questions from a grayhaired boss in a small, dark office. "We're expanding," he said. "We want to hit the youth market—and that's you." I was hired. I would work in Europe, putting tours together, after I learned the business. My mother met the news with a look of mingled ecstasy and fear. I was leaving. But I was marketable. So was she. She'd found work on her own; now I'd done the same.

A golden light shone on the rest of that vacation, and the big world seemed so close. I met the famous cellist Mstislav Rostropovich at the Goodmans', where he was staying. We had lunch on their terrace in the mild St. Louis air, under the enormous oak tree—Alice and I and "Slava," with his round face and the aureole of hair around his bald head. He still lived in Russia and was in danger there for sheltering the dissident Aleksandr Solzhenitsyn in his dacha. "How brave he is," I thought, "but how mischievous!" Was that how it was with great men? He sniffed hugely at the food—he was on a diet, but made a great show of savoring what he couldn't eat. "I enjoy—like this," he said in his broken English, sniffing and laughing.

I wanted to be like him—full-tilt alive; serious but silly. We were already trying for that mix in the little youth society that had formed in our house. The evening before we left for Alabama my brother Judd and I and our temporary brother Greig stood around in a hollow of the hill below the back porch in the chilly twilight where we couldn't be seen, smoking a joint, shivering, murmuring, giggling. Later we called Harry and Mardy to a special session in Greig's room that had once been Maidie's—up the back stairs, in that always mysterious part of the house. We put Tracy Nelson, singing "Down So Low," on Greig's record player. "It's about loneliness, and life and everything," we told our eager brother and sister. "I've learned how to give now/But what good will that do?" wailed Tracy in her gospel-tinged voice, banging away ham-fistedly on the piano. "No one can touch me-e-e-e . . . the way you used to do." It was so sad, but so thrilling. There was a roving life up ahead—in all the world capitals—full of people who set other people on fire, and then left holes in their hearts.

Tomorrow morning we were going south because my mother had finally acknowledged the life of the body. Everything was coming together. Nothing was wrong. Every mile would bring us closer to the ocean, and to the sun.

G ODDAMN IT, BETTY, YOU CAN'T FIT ALL THIS STUFF
in the car," my father was shouting at my mother, as we all tried to
load suitcases, bundles, backpacks, book bags, purses, and my
brother's guitar into the Volkswagen Rabbit, which stood, lit up
with all its doors open, outside the front door. We were starting
the trip in the pitch-dark before dawn. My father wasn't coming
with us because of a sales luncheon at his job, though he was flying down later that evening. But he was supervising the packing.
And he was driven to distraction, as usual, by our disorderliness.

As we drove off he was still avoiding our looks. I thought it
was the start of another of the lengthy blanks in my parents' relationship, but my mother backed the car down the driveway again,
got out, and put her arms around his neck.

"Old Jack, old grump," she said, making a face of mock woe
toward us in the car windows. She hung on him a little, then got

back into the car and off we drove again, leaving him standing alone in his bathrobe as the first peach-colored light touched the front door.

Inside the car we settled into silence as our neighborhood slipped by, houses and churches still closed up for the night. I read my mother the directions for the route in a low voice. When we got on the highway I glanced at her—she was staring anxiously ahead, thinking her own thoughts, so I sank down in my seat and watched out the window.

People in a car lose their wants, their essential colors, like packages of dried food which become eggs or peas or apple pie only when water is added at the end of the journey. I was numb in the front passenger seat. Clouds had covered the sky; the light showed as a crack at the horizon. Wide, flat fields flashed by, and patches of woods and muddy farms. In the backseat Judd, Harry, and Mardy were tucked into postures of exhaustion, and in the luggage compartment, Sam lay with his feet up on the window.

We stopped a few hours later when someone spotted a turquoise Stuckey's awning and a sign that promised free pecan divinity with a tank of gas. Free candy! Anything to cut the boredom. "I think you'd better take the wheel," said my mother, yawning, to me. "I didn't get to bed till late because of last-minute things." I got out of the car to wake up. A cold rain was falling. I did a few calisthenics. That's when impatience took over. Somewhere down the road—it could be five minutes, it could be five hours—the cold would just end, and spring would begin. This was a version of my father's temper: an unbearable itch to have it the way my body had projected.

The skinny kid who had filled our gas tank came running out with the candy. I put the box on the seat between me and my mother and opened it as we drove out, so anyone could take some. The candy studded with nuts imprinted itself on my mind: those nuts slashed in the middle, exposing their white insides.

The rain kept on; it was the superhighway that ended. A two-lane road took over where it stopped. It wasn't so bad, I thought: just straight and flat, though I faced what one always faces when exiting a superhighway—a pinch of fright at the possible nearness of cars coming the other way. Beside me, my mother had leaned back and gone instantly to sleep. She looked like a child. She must have been tired. The rain was relentless. The windshield wipers slapped back and forth in front of me. I checked the kids in the rearview mirror. They had their noses and hands pressed flat against the cold glass, while drops of rain snaked back along the windows.

It would be sunset when we got there. We would tumble out of the car onto the warm sand, then we would race down to the sea to taste it. In the morning we would lie on the beach with our eyes closed; the sun would dissolve us into little particles and the salt water would shock us back into our bodies. I would return to college radiant. I sat up straighter and pressed down the gas pedal. If we went 65 mph instead of 60, release from this hell of a rainfall would be quicker.

That's when the truck appeared in the distance. The road sloped imperceptibly down. The low walls of a little bridge could be seen farther on, but the wide gray truck coming toward me on the other side of the road was closer. I braked. The truck shook as it passed and splashed a slew of water on my windshield. I saw waves of water. The windshield cleared a second later to reveal the bridge looming ahead and the dark water of the stream, as if a giant hand had flicked us onto another course. There was no time to name the sight; the riverbank fed itself to my eyes; the bridge wall met the hurtling car.

WHEN I BEGAN to see again, it was intermittently, through a haze of pulsing yellow dots. Thinking was slow. Was I awake? I was constrained. The steering wheel was pressing into my stomach, and the driver's seat felt like a case built to fit my hunched form. But the gray daylight wouldn't go away; it stayed.

Outside was Judd, who bent in at the window to show a face gashed purple under the eyes. "Can you get out?" he asked.

"How did *you* get out?" I asked confusedly. He had been behind me in the car. Maybe he had floated out above my head while I slept with the steering wheel in my arms. I had forgotten there were doors.

"But *Mom.* Look at Mom." Judd was staring into the car beyond me and I turned my head to see what I had already sensed. My mother sat unmoving in the seat to the right of me. Her head lolled to the side like a person asleep on a bus, but her throat was bathed in blood. She had a dumb expression on her face; she wasn't hearing.

"Get me out," I said in a daze, turning my head back to Judd. "What about the others?"

"The others are all right, I think," Judd said as he tugged me and I inched my way free of the crushed driver's seat.

Outside, the rain had lightened. I stumbled over the deep tire tracks made by our car and realized that my clammy vision came from blood flowing down my own face. I found the wound above my eye, then blotted it with the hem of my dress.

"Oh, catch Harry!" I cried as my tall, skinny brother stumbled ahead of me. His legs didn't seem to know how to walk. Mardy, with mud on her face and in her blond hair, leaned against the car, staring; beyond her, little Sam was walking in circles and asking if this was the worst day in the world. I brought him to Mardy and attached their hands together, then I limped to the roadside where a dark green car had stopped and a man in a gray business suit was talking to Judd.

"Could you help us, please?" I said to the man through slow lips. "We must have an ambulance immediately for my mother," I added, in case Judd had been talking about something else.

"Now, why don't you just sit down here in the car and rest. The ambulance is on the way," the man said, staring at me.

"No, thank you, I can walk," I assured him, touching my crooked face. I tried to look straight into his eyes to convince him I could walk, but I missed them and saw only his thinning hair and red forehead.

Back around the twisted Volkswagen I hobbled and bent down to the bloody, loose-faced form of my mother in the front seat. What should I do—try artificial respiration? Lay her down? I didn't want to touch her at all, because I knew the head would fall off in my arms. So I just sniffed at her body. My cheek was near hers, and it was quiet there.

Sirens. I straightened up to see the white-coated hospital men running in my direction with a stretcher, while beyond them the ambulance light flashed on and on. It was a black ambulance. Why had they sent a black ambulance? The town of Hayti, Missouri, had no ambulances, it turned out, so they used the hearse.

More cars had stopped by the road and a small crowd of people had gathered, some of whom were leading the children to the ambulance. "Please"—I grabbed an arm of a sandy-haired medic— "take my mother first. She might die. Come back for us."

He nodded. A woman led me gently by the shoulders to the front seat of the ambulance, where the other kids were piled in, waiting. We waited a terribly long time. I tried to get out again, but the medics were loading my mother into the wounded person's place in the back, and finally the big black car tore off down the road to the rising pitch of its siren. None of us could look back at the stretcher for more than a second. We were inside the wail of the siren, fixed on the forward speed of the vehicle.

It was a little brick hospital on the highway, which said "Hayti, Missouri" in chrome letters above the door. Its hall inside was cool and linoleum-modern, with the alcohol smell of a hospital corridor and white-coated personnel arriving from all sides on padded shoes. We limped in behind our mother's stretcher, like a ragged army. One of the nurses gasped and put a fist to her mouth. The stretcher was spirited away through a door in the back, and we were led off one by one to be treated for our wounds.

"Judd, stay with them," I whispered and broke away to approach a tall, blue-coated man. He confirmed that he was the doctor. I told him I could hear the truth without falling apart. He put his hand on my shoulder: she was dead. I whipped my head around toward the door where the stretcher had disappeared.

"I'd better make phone calls right away," I said. "I can walk."

The room was cool, and it contained one green-blottered desk on which a black telephone sat. I dialed my father's office. Do I say "I'm afraid something terrible has happened?" I wondered, but when I heard his voice, I said it brutally in two sentences, "We had a car accident. Mom's dead," which brought a silence, then violent sobs from him. There was a scuffle in the background, and my uncle, his boss, came on the phone. They would charter a plane; they would be there as soon as they could.

"Stay with me, operator," I said. Operator? Scalpel? Pincers? My mind was going giddy. Where was I? My home city spread out in my imagination, and I started on the list of relatives who had to be told. A nurse came silently into the room, sat down, and offered her hand, which I took and gripped tightly. "Of those so close beside me, which are you?" That was by Theodore Roethke; I'd memorized it at Mary Institute. "God bless the Ground! I shall walk softly there. . . ."

The thought of my grandmother came to me—alone, probably in her living room, seated at the piano. Someone else should tell her, a person, not a telephone. My psychiatrist uncle, married to my youngest aunt. He came on the phone.

I followed my own stiff and limping progress through the halls of the little country hospital—*Captain Ahab. No, I'm not searching for something, I've lost something. Are those two things the same? I'm playing with words. Maybe this is Emily Dickinson's formal feeling after great pain,* I thought, lying alone in the small room of blue linoleum where they'd brought me, but then the thought of the other body lying in another room, with no thoughts now, seized me like a spasm. It was a body already; its mind had collapsed like a lung. Tears slipped out at the sides of my eyes and around the back of my head. I wanted to tell the doctor looming in the space above me how good it was that some of the linoleum in the room was blue instead of white, but I thought he might take that confidence as a sign of hysteria, so I didn't say anything. I'd better watch myself, I thought, other people don't know about the little things, the sounds and the colors. The pain as he felt my knee caused me to float above the table, and I didn't even realize when he began cleaning the cut above my eye. He was saying something I couldn't catch, then I heard "there'll be a scar."

Bandaged, on my feet, and steadied by the crutches in my armpits, I surveyed my family from the threshhold of the little white room where some maternal person had thought to put us all. The kids were ranged around the room on two beds and a wheelchair, all in white smocks, looking up at me like an audience.

"You all know?" I asked.

"Yes," said Judd, camouflaged by a large white turban.

"Judd the pasha," I blurted out, then announced more quietly that we were now a band, as in band of adventurers.

"To the end," said Harry.

"Sam, is your knee all right?" I asked him, looking at the wheelchair.

"Well," he said in his most precocious seven-year-old voice, "the doctor says I'm usurping one of the hospital's key wheelchairs for a flesh wound," which caused all of us to grin stupidly.

"But he has to practice," said Judd. "He's going to be the first star soccer offense in a wheelchair."

"Zippo on wheels, they'll call him," Harry continued, as Sam let out a kind of drooling giggle in spite of himself. "He'll develop special lap muscles for catching and throwing."

"He'll make us famous," I said, hobbling over to sit on a bed, "along with Mardy, who shall now be the family musician. We must have one, and thank God it's a cello with deep tones. Harry the master builder," I continued the story.

"And court jester," said Harry.

"Thank you," I said, "and Judd the brilliant legal mind. Sam—you still have time to figure all this out. Where does that leave me?"

"The chief?" said Harry.

"The chief what?" I asked.

"The chief actor," Judd said. "We have to act out the magic for a while. You're the one who knows what to do."

I leaned my head on the hard wall, which was already supporting my back, and looked at them all. Here we were, contained for one more moment in the eyes of a dead person. The accident wasn't the explosion. This was the explosion, now. We couldn't hear it or see it, but it was happening as we sat here—drawing us up together in its terrible force. I could almost see our souls, in white hospital gowns, rising on the hot wind and dancing together under the ceiling.

THE MOOD OF EXHILARATION PERSISTED ALL DAY IN the hospital, that giddy exhilaration that comes from knowing there's a void opening up beneath one's every action.

We joked brilliantly with the nurses. We lavished affection on the town's red-faced chief banker bearing flowers—my uncle had telephoned him to look in on us. When my father came in at the end of the day behind my uncle, we clustered around him. "I'll try to be both father and mother to you," he said in a choked voice. Then we drove on a series of rural highways to the little airport where my father and uncle had landed in the chartered plane. The sun came out suddenly on a green landscape and gilded a boy and a dog standing by the side of the road. Tomorrow was Good Friday; then would come Easter. The world had flushed out into beauty—too early, too late.

We flew north, back into rainy skies that turned to evening and then night as we landed. At the end of our driveway, no dark and empty house loomed up as I had feared. Cars were parked everywhere. Where had they come from? The front door was open, light was streaming out, people were moving about inside, putting food on the dining room table. It was all the "aunts" and "uncles" of my childhood, my parents' oldest friends, I saw as we limped into the house, the ones from whom my mother had been lately estranged. Their faces loomed up, bathed in familiarity yet off-kilter, as in a lens. Aunt Ellen, standing by the table, supervising . . . the bulk of her, the redness of her face—so known, so strange. Another "aunt" face from my childhood was loudly regretting an argument she'd had recently with my mother about Negroes.

The younger kids were groggy and dazed. Sam curled up on a corner of the couch and went to sleep. Harry and Mardy just sat, and Judd with his head bandage was warily polite. But I waded into the throng, hugging, acknowledging, meeting each eye with the glad recognition my mother would have summoned. I had jumped into my mother's skin; I was swelling up with human charity. It was a primal response to what had happened. If I filled up her place, it wouldn't be empty. At the same time, metaphysical thoughts were coursing through my mind, as if my intellect were scrambling to detach itself from the present horror and latch onto those steady friends, history and geography. *All this food,* I thought, *but no one is hungry. . . . So it's a symbol . . . like an ancient offering . . . fruits of the earth . . . offered to death . . . Kentucky Fried Chicken? . . . What a joke. . . . Synthetic fruits—hormone-fed. . . . Somehow the right thing. . . . My mother would be proud of her people . . .*

The next day grew more disjointed. Among the dispropor-
tionate impulses that swam into my head came one to exhort my
sister to continue her cello, as my mother would have wished, by
means of Rostropovich. He was still in town. With the lèse-
majesté of catastrophe I called up the Goodmans. They were
shocked to hear my voice. "But we were waiting to call you.
Come right over," they said. "Slava didn't sleep all night after
hearing what happened." I drove there with my sister in tow. Rostropovich came bounding out of the Goodmans' house like a
great bear and enfolded us both in his arms, and rocked us and
cried with us. "Fate arranged to have him here for us," said my
feverish thoughts, "fate brought him all the way from Russia. Fate
sent me another mother, for just an instant, in the body of a big,
emotional man."

Indeed, with Rostropovich, the high-pitched mental fever in
my brain subsided for a moment. The force of affection that
poured from this great musician, with his aureole of gray hair and
his face screwed up in outrage, put everything back where it belonged. I became human in his embrace and began to sob.

Rostropovich did give my sister a cello lesson, which marked
her awkwardly in local circles as a genius (my poor sister, who
had wanted to play the harp, not the cello). But it is his concern
for me that I remember. He carefully asked me what I was going
to do. *I'm going back to Boston, to college.* For an instant I glimpsed
the utter bleakness of continuing with my life as it had been laid
out before. Then his face bent down. "I am your papa," he said to
me. "I will call friend, in Boston, to take care of you."

At the funeral, too, just the edge of that darkness could be felt,
the darkness that would soon overtake us all. It was held at the
bright redbrick suburban church my mother had loved. We filed

from a side door into the front row, in our mourning clothes and our knee and head bandages. A huge throng of black and white faces looked back at us—all the different circles of friends—with more people pushing behind them to get in. Two hundred people couldn't find a place and waited outside during the service. The simple pine coffin stood alone on the steps to the altar.

Words were intoned. An old Easter hymn was sung, "The strife is o'er, the battle done / The victory of life is won. . . ." Easter was a day away. Wasn't it like my mother to die at Easter? Once again everything clashed in my mind: the hope of resurrection, the nothingness of death. This was her hymn. She'd believed what it said. She'd been a fighter; she'd conquered worlds of prejudice. But she must have been so tired. So many people had impinged on her imagination with their needs. She'd taken care of them—and of us too, her children. And of people who didn't give her enough, like my father. She'd never allowed herself any visible melancholy.

"The song of triumph has begun: Alleluia!" went the hymn. What was that victory and that triumph? Was it that you could finally rest?

A WEEK AFTER the accident Judd and I flew back to college. No one blamed me for what had happened. The police never asked for my story of conditions on the road. No family member ever suggested out loud that I'd been driving too fast and caused the whole thing. But the thought that I was my mother's murderer flickered in the recesses of my own being. I left it there. Had these been ordinary times, grief and guilt might have come in a natural sequence. In my dorm room at night, under the many-paned tall window, I might have sobbed and retched and gotten some of it out. But times were not ordinary at American colleges.

On the day we flew into Boston, April 10, the university exploded in the strike of 1969. Such an event had been a long time coming, on the heels of the ever-escalating Vietnam war. At a place like Harvard, the tangle of privilege and protest, guilt and entitlement, had lent extra urgency to the antiwar movement. There had been the McNamara incident in 1966, when the defense secretary was imprisoned in his car; the tomato attack on a Dow Chemical recruiter in 1967; the student occupation of Paine Hall in 1968, where the faculty was to have had a meeting on the fate of ROTC, the military unit on campus.

Now, on April 9, 1969, the day before Judd and I flew back, came another building takeover. Three hundred students occupied Harvard's main administration building, University Hall, roughing up some deans and making free with the furniture. The ostensible cause was the continuing existence of ROTC, plus Harvard's record as a landlord in working-class Cambridge, along with the black students' demand for a black studies department. Negotiations might have ensued had not Harvard's president, Nathan Pusey, called in the riot police the next morning to evict the students. In the predawn hours of April 10, a half day before our return, a crowd of city police swarmed into Harvard Yard in their blue helmets, wielding nightsticks and tear gas; they routed the students from University Hall and beat some of them up. Judd and I heard about it on the cab radio, driving in from the airport.

"Blood here too?" I thought wearily. Crowds were milling when we stopped at Harvard Yard to let my brother out. At my own dorm, talk boiled over in the corridors. The next day I went along in a tide of people to a meeting at the football stadium, where shouting and seizing of the microphone went on, with high-pitched rhetoric punctuated by bursts of cheering.

Death had shifted gears and become mass action; there wasn't even a pause for loneliness. Judd still had a bandaged head—people assumed he'd been in University Hall. I was a restless presence in strike meetings because my own American History and Lit graduate-student teachers were strike leaders, especially big, blond Barry O'Connell, who had commanded the microphone at the Soldiers' Field rally. I can see myself sitting silent on top of a desk in the midst of one of those meetings, whipping my head around to catch every eye, looking into every face with a combination of wonder and terrible need. Otherwise, I raced all over Cambridge on a bicycle, to the "alternative seminars" that had replaced our canceled classes, wearing the strike's red armband on my right arm.

Graduation brought an end to this frenzied activity. Despite the strike, they let us graduate, in caps and gowns, proceeding over the fresh green grass of Radcliffe Yard. It was more a rite of passage than we knew: besides being the class of the strike, we would be the last Radcliffe class to graduate separate from Harvard. Amid the throng of relatives on the sidelines stood my people: my father, my brother, my tutor Ann, my aunt Dodie from Princeton (tearfully representing my mother), and my paternal grandparents down from New Hampshire. The grandparents spent the ceremony debating sotto voce what the red armbands meant and concluded they were badges for cum laude.

IN JUNE I came home and went to work for Open Road, the travel company that had hired me in the spring. The company's boss was astonished that I should still want the job after the accident. But I'd seen the alternative in one of those flashes of a possible future. It would be so easy to move back home, live in my old room, send my brothers and sisters off to school, eat midnight dinners with my father . . . The logic of it terrified me—especially the mental picture of those dinners with my father. Some part of me wanted them. I had to get out.

I started in Open Road's home office "learning the business," which meant typing with the secretaries, until I reminded the boss in my most winning manner that I was supposed to work in Europe. So they printed out a ticket for me. I spent the rest of the summer and fall commuting in an endless loop among London, Paris, and Rome, but no one told me what to do. My company, once a fine-tuned luxury tour operation, had gone public, received a flood of capital, hired new employees, and jumped into the business of mass packaged tours without quite knowing the sequence of development. I tried to make city diagrams and work plans and took copious notes on youth activities. The bosses flew over to Europe for meetings with their European partners, held excitedly in cozy French bistros and rustic Italian trattorias. They flew me in, too, from wherever I was making my notes, to lend my amusing opinions to the mix. Should they buy hotels; should they pitch to new markets? I knew nothing of this. The head boss liked to have me around as a good-luck charm.

So I focused all my manic energies on this group of slightly seedy men, who tried lasciviously to comfort me at night in hotel corridors, except for Karl, the pale and bitter young German in the double-breasted navy suit. In my bewilderment I attached myself to the lonely Karl, who fled when he could at the sight of me, though I succumbed to the advances of a fat, red-haired, aftershave-scented Dane because he was "a kind man," as I wrote in my journal.

In between these meetings, an addiction to solitude was growing in me. Or rather, it was a slippage between surface and depths. Part of me was jabbering on and flirting; the other part was wandering the streets and swallowing lights, dusk, cathedrals, museums, silhouettes of balconies, faces of passersby, as if they were landmarks for a drowning person. My mother's death still seemed too huge a fact to focus on, so I let it hang like a terrible moon in the dark sky of my being. I could feel myself slipping, slipping into the silence.

I carried a primitive tape recorder in my luggage and some rock-and-roll tapes to guard against loneliness. But the songs were all about loneliness. Stevie Winwood of Blind Faith wailed in a disembodied voice that he couldn't find his way home. All the electric guitars screamed in another song, the drums erupted, and Winwood's voice rose again in an apocalyptic whine, "Have to cry today. . . ." It seemed you were supposed to cry, but crying by yourself made it worse. In a Piccadilly Circus movie house I saw Peter Fonda and Dennis Hopper set out in *Easy Rider,* in their motorcycle-armchairs, on those endless roads of the American West. These hippies hadn't all lost their mothers, not that I knew of. But they might as well have, since they'd disowned them.

I was in the center, at any rate, of that angry and mournful zeitgeist, even if I hadn't put myself there on purpose. I was shunning my home and mourning it too, just like all the singer-poets—Dylan, Winwood, the Beatles . . . Or rather, I didn't have a home, since there was no home without my mother. Most of the time I just felt sick with numbness, sick of asking myself so many times a day what it was that I wanted. Wandering the seedy little streets of Notting Hill Gate, I longed for a clean life empty of all the furnishings. I longed to be rid of these middle-aged men of Open Road who ate too much and drank too much. California was the place to start over. Ellen Mandel was in Berkeley; she'd written that I could stay with her. I resolved to quit my job.

But first I had to go back to St. Louis for my father's wedding.

IN NOVEMBER A letter had come to me from my father, in care of Open Road London. "Recently met a most lovely gal I am infatuated with. She's great and we have much fun and good times together. Her name is Jean Hamburg and she has 3 children, one girl 23 working and a son at Stanford and one at U. of Wisconsin. She knew Betty." My father, up till then, had been trying to do what he'd promised: be both mother and father. This letter itself was one of the warmest I ever got from him. He told me his own news in it, he thanked me in his usual terse style for my "nice letters and gifts to the family," and informed me "All kids coming along, with Harry and Mardy in real demand with the young people. Really something to see."

But being the ur-parent hadn't been enough to fill up the blankness in my father, which must have been greater than my own. When Jean appeared with her exotic aura (she was Jewish), her enlightened emotional demands, her chic social life, and her remodeled downtown row house with the master bedroom "floating" over the living room, Henry moved himself over to her life, and he walked out of his. The hawk-breeding project fell into disarray; other falconers came at his invitation and took away the grow lights, the perches, the one-way window, even the once-precious falcon chicks that had hatched just before the accident. After a while my father didn't even sleep at the old house.

When I came home in December, fourteen- and fifteen-year-olds were wandering the halls; a sweet marijuana smell clung to the back stairs; the Rolling Stones blared from the stereo in the living room that used to be forbidden to children. Our house, already part commune when my mother was alive, had gone all the way. The atmosphere, though, was upbeat. My brother Harry was the den mother of this impromptu tribe; he was now a long-haired high school junior with an Indian-style bandanna just like his older brother's. He'd made a temporary headquarters in my room, which was hung with batik cloths and yarn "god's-eyes" woven on crossed sticks. He and Mardy, a blond hippie angel in a short dashiki, were managing the house. They'd learned a lot since they'd first gone food shopping and come home with parsley, sage, rosemary, thyme, and a watermelon. Now they shopped and cooked like grown-ups, and sent Sam off to school in the mornings.

Little Sam, alone upstairs in Harry and Judd's old room, was masquerading as a robot. He walked with stiff arms and answered "Af-firmative" when you asked if he wanted to go outside. "It's a creative response to the situation," I thought with a vague and distant guilt. Nobody dared tell me I should be there myself, caring for my little brother, making sure he was loved and looked after. If they'd said that, I could have explained my actions, told them I couldn't face coming back, that I had to make my own life. Instead, I was welcomed home as a figurehead of the new order, an authentic wanderer, a rock-and-roll connoisseur. My room was returned with a flourish.

This wild and scrappy life was about to end, though. When my father and Jean got engaged, they decided to sell our house and move into hers. I wasn't present for this decision. I'd given Open Road the month in St. Louis I thought was their due, then quit and gone back East to play at being a faculty wife in Newark, Delaware, where my old boyfriend Cruce was a young professor. Of this Delaware time I remember only the moments when I fell asleep at faculty parties, in spare rooms, on piles of coats.

While I was away, the B'nai B'rith ladies invited by Jean cleaned out all the closets and the attic of the old house and held a yard sale in the driveway. I didn't get to say good-bye to the things or the house. When I returned in February 1970, home was Jean's house, with its bright-white stairways, its rooms at different levels, its chic bleached rugs in the living room, its master bedroom, where everything could be heard from downstairs, its two small rooms on the top floor, where we siblings slept like sardines. Jean was nice, with sad brown eyes, but so lost in her own melancholy that she got upset when Harry and Mardy refused to call her Mom. Little Sam, though, cheerfully obliged.

On the day of the wedding it was snowing. We siblings and our new stepsiblings piled into Jean's station wagon to go to her mother's apartment. My father was driving. As he pulled out of the back alley into the street, he stopped the car. He and Buzzy, Jean's tall dark son, usually the kindest boy—I was half in love with him—jumped out of the car and wrestled fiercely in the light of the headlights, sliding all over the street in the snow. I didn't know why it happened—maybe they'd left an argument unfinished. But it didn't matter why they were fighting. I was in that dreamy observer state in which nothing quite mattered. *It's an Oedipal struggle,* I thought with distant interest. *Buzzy must think my father has stolen his mother.*

This would have been the moment to say to my father "Wait! Stop! What are you doing with your life? With her life? With all our lives?" But none of us had the presence of mind to do this. Instead, we waded into this wedding with manic cheer. A white-tiered cake stood on Jean's mother's dining room table. New cousins and aunts, all with those sad brown eyes, waited around. The new grandmother was tall and stern-looking, like my grandmother Kendall. But she had a warm, sharp look on her face, or that's how I phrased it to myself. She had grown up an orphan, Jean had said. She loved music. She had given me a Mozart record for Christmas. Maybe this instant new family wouldn't be so bad.

But I left again before I could find out. I left for California with one of my new stepcousins, Jean's nephew John Schwab, an inarticulate young man who happened to be driving west in an old Mercedes. We crossed Missouri, Oklahoma, New Mexico, Arizona, California. We were mostly silent. When the landscape turned to desert, I made him stop by some of the red boulders on the roadside, so I could sit on them and put my face to the sun.

"I'm healing," I said to myself. "This is the beginning of getting better." But I was just getting emptier. When we hit Death Valley I had the sudden urge to do a handstand. John Schwab, ever polite, scrambled up a mountain and photographed me as a tiny, upside-down figure, alone in a vast, salt-scarred landscape.

IN CALIFORNIA, time ran out on my pretense of holding normal conversations and making coherent decisions. I couldn't talk to anyone. The wrongness of my remaining alive in suspended animation while my mother was dead had overcome me. She would be accomplishing reams of things—mothering her children, integrating her city; I was doing nothing. I lived in the spare room of a white house in Berkeley that my former roommate was renting. Ellen was starting a new life, with piano lessons and a boyfriend who'd been high up in the writing world, at *Newsweek*. Then he'd dropped out to be a musician in a rock band. Such a famous thing as *Newsweek* quashed me utterly. I wore the same dress every day, a loose one of thin-waled blue corduroy, on the bodice of which I had crudely stitched, in pink yarn, a couplet from the old Shaker song that I thought could serve as an all-purpose motto: "When true simplicity is gained / To bow and to bend we shan't be ashamed." But the yarn had shrunk in the wash and the words were an indecipherable pink scribble.

In that hippie pilgrimage site of Berkeley, California, boxes of clothes stood on street corners. You could trade your old clothes for someone else's. Woozy camaraderie spilled from any casual encounter. I was as lost inside as I would ever be. I worked part-time at a health-food café beside skinny young hippies in stained aprons. I remember the vat of dark lentil mix called "dal," into which I stared while trying not to cry. I can remember flashes of the visions brought on by LSD and mescaline during camping trips. The Pacific palisades flickered purple. The shadows along a mountain trail dripped with snake shapes. A leather ring I wore signaled blood; a bracelet of blue beads meant sky.

There are flashes as well of real journeys. I was constantly leaving Berkeley to hitchhike up and down the California coast, pursuing love affairs and friendships I can barely remember. One dark night I stood alone with my thumb out at the crossroads of two superhighways frequented by trucks. At that moment I saw myself as if from above, a being already dissolved in the night and the roar. I saw that I was trying to die.

After that night on the highway I took some practical steps to salvage myself. I went back East. Using money I'd saved from Open Road, and a student loan, I got a degree from Harvard to be an English teacher (my mother had said teaching was a safe profession). I took up modern dance, which seemed to address the speed sickness I knew still lodged in my body after the accident. I taught and studied dance in Boston, then I went to France to attend a summer dance course. I lingered in Paris, where I'd once felt so gay and free on my school trip. I applied to a Parisian pantomime school to "discover my inner clown." To pay for mime school I got a part-time secretarial job in Paris, at the American University. Then I changed my mind about the pantomime and the clown, got on an overnight train to Marseilles and begged admission to a physical culture institute in that city, one that was supposed to teach me who I was through body-imaging.

None of these plans concerned my real need, which was for comfort and pity and a safe place to grieve in. But I wasn't reachable even if someone had tried to comfort me. The people of those years give off a strange aura in memory, when they are remembered—as if the grinding of my need against my detachment has set off poisonous sparks around their images.

One day on a rainy Paris street in the fall of 1973, I decided to fly home to New York, though New York wasn't my home. Freud had said love and work were the main things. The love was beyond me; the work I could address. New York, that scary city of ambition, seemed the right place to find it. From the airport I phoned Ann Douglas, my college adviser, now in Princeton. She said I was an answer to her prayers; she was ending her marriage. Get on a bus and come, she said.

At three the next morning in her kitchen, preternaturally awake from jet lag, I heated some milk for café au lait and began to teach myself to write, translating an article about women's eating habits from French *Elle*. I didn't know it then, but I had lurched onto a path that would restore me to life. Each article, each book, would buy my life back from death, because it was a thing I'd made, and it was worth something.

THROUGH ALL THIS time and afterward, my mother came to me in my dreams. Or else I summoned her. In the months after the accident she appeared in the dreams radiant, smiling, and pregnant—the opposite of dead. Such dreams brought impersonal comfort, like religious visitations. Then the numbness set in, which took years to lift, and the dreams got grimmer. My mother hadn't died, she'd gone away of her own free will. In one dream she had married again but her second husband was dead, and now she had reappeared to throw herself on the mercy of my father. In another she'd been in prison. Now she was out and living with an unpleasant woman who monitored her phone calls and didn't like her to talk to us.

Or she'd been in self-imposed exile in Europe, like the lonely Countess Olenska in Edith Wharton's *Age of Innocence,* or in a commune for the simpleminded, the kind that let you out only if they were sure of you. The commune dream took place at our country club swimming pool, where I was trying to show my mother a swan dive from the high board so she could see how free I'd grown. But I got scared; I climbed down from the diving board. And she was losing interest. Harry and I tried to kidnap her in that dream, the way they used to kidnap brainwashed people from the Moonies' religious cult. I realized, still inside the dream, that no place was left in our lives for my mother: we were all grown, my father had remarried—twice by 1983, when I had this dream. So I let her go back to her commune people on the other side of the pool, with whom she was happier.

My role in these dreams was strange. I wasn't exactly my mother's daughter. I was some kind of mediator, trying to shield my mother from the knowledge that we'd all gone on living without her; trying in some impulsive way to include her in my present life. Or I was her lover, holding her by the sheer force of my presence to the world she'd abandoned. Of course the dreams didn't let me do that; they knew she was already dead.

In the Ellen Olenska dream, my mother's return from exile found us brothers and sisters all together in our red Volkwagen bus in New Hampshire. She was sad because her second husband had left her. She was driving us on a beautiful mountain road with a view into the distance. Everybody's spouses and partners were with us, and I was in the passenger seat. I leaned over and gave my mother a long kiss, then I reached for the wheel, because the passion of that kiss had made us so breathless that driving was difficult. That dream ended in suspense: would we crash?

There were questions posed in these dreams that I couldn't yet answer: whether my mother and I had been too close; whether I could live a normal life without her. My mother got strangely mixed up with Faith in some of the dreams, playing the role of a forgotten member of the family to whom nobody was paying enough attention. Faith died in 1982 at twenty-four, of respiratory failure. She hadn't grown physically for many years; she was still small at the end, like a child. She'd been living in an Illinois farm home for the retarded, unvisited by anyone but Mardy, because none of the others of us could bear it. My father went to see her on her hospital deathbed. He said that her face was smoothed out at last from that pinched anguish, and she looked as normal as you or me.

Perhaps it was Faith's death that enhanced for a while the morbidity of my thoughts about my mother. Sometime in the eighties, dreams and waking thoughts began to coalesce in a theory that my mother had died because she was tired of living; that fatigue, or grief for Faith, or failure of nerve, or the longing for heaven had pulled her in the late sixties off the life track.

It is true that my mother died at the moment when the habit of hoping for a better world died in the wider culture. Martin Luther King Jr. and Robert Kennedy had both been assassinated in 1968, the year before our accident. It was never possible to believe again, after they were gone, that social intervention could make people altruists. The question arose in my mind: had King's and Kennedy's deaths weakened my mother's hold on life? Had she arranged in her unconscious mind to follow them into martyrdom? When my mother's old school friend Nancy Painter went through her papers, she reported that all her projects seemed finished.

Then, too, my mother had almost died once before, when Faith was born. The doctor had restored her to life on that occasion by calling her name. At the accident no one had called her name. Could it be that she had rushed back willingly into the heavenly tunnel of light she'd seen once before—and through it to that other land?

The evidence for all this is quite flimsy. If I try to remember any indication that my mother wanted to stop living, I can't find one. The presumption of her failed will to live existed only in my dreams, or in a reckless habit I sometimes entertained of blurring thought by invoking fate. Perhaps I created my mother's need to die in my numb years, when my mind was casting about to explain the loss it had been forced to absorb in one violent moment. Perhaps I manufactured a congenital death wish in my mother so I could be angry at her while maintaining my own privileged condition of being alive. If I was angry at my mother for wanting to die, I didn't have to be angry at myself for causing her death.

But if the opposite was true, if my mother hadn't wanted to die and I hadn't wanted her dead, that meant her death was caused after all by pure chance, by a roll of the dice—by an exact confluence of the atoms of matter that caused our car to meet up with that truck, on that rainy road, at that fatal moment in the spring of 1969.

THE PROBLEM IS that I can't let her be meaninglessly gone, like one of the poet Rilke's "countless, silent dead," crowded together just beyond the horizon of what we can see. The being-that-was-my-mother must stand out. She must have an identity out there in that undiscovered country of the air. And it's not the identity of a singing teacher up in heaven, helping other dead people sing in harmony, as a kindly woman medium seemed to think when I went for a consultation. The woman held a silver ring I wear while she concentrated—to have contact with me, she explained—and asked me to say my mother's name out loud while she got in touch with her. Is that how heaven files them, by name?

In life my mother refused to see herself as a solo figure. She saw herself as a part of the people around her. She was a perpetual mother of her own young children, and of all retarded children. She was a friend and coworker and a social visionary who kept trying to bring disparate populations together. Above all she was a daughter—of her parents, her city, her country, who kept on believing, daughter-like, in a parental and national ideal. And I, the daughter of that daughter, caught with her in the too-tight space of her visions and her beliefs, kept scuffling to get free of that daughterhood: to become cynical and scornful and disbelieving and unreverential. But I couldn't do it while she was alive. We were wound too tightly around each other, even as we were both growing and trying, in our separate ways, to uncoil from each other.

Then the thread that connected us—the thread that bound my mother to life—was cut, and she went soaring off into the air, and I landed on the ground. I have made a life that is in every way the opposite of hers. I'm not a daughter (except to my father—sort of), and I'm not a mother. I live alone in the city of Manhattan, which is as far from my mother's version of a community as there can be in this country. I earn my own living. I define myself by my work. I am as much an extreme example of my generation as she was of hers. Her generation threw itself into raising families and merging with families; mine has insisted on the right to be solo. Mine is the first female generation in Western history to explore en masse the possibility of having a career and living alone.

Other women in my generation, though, have had the chance to ease into their work-driven lives still in contact with their mothers. Some of the mothers have even started their own work lives; and the daughters have become mothers and produced children of their own. But between my mother's life, which I grew up in, and my present life, there was no overlap. Death made a gulf. We weren't ever adults together, growing and changing side by side, talking about things and bending to each other's opinions.

So maybe I am not the one who can make sense of my mother as a dead person. I wasn't able to recover her spirit intact for many years, despite the dreams she wandered through. Instead, a darkness flowered in the deep place she occupied inside my psyche while she was alive. Sometimes, even now, I will be crossing a street, or getting out of a cab at an airport, or sitting with my tax papers like a competent adult, and pure shock overtakes me that my mother isn't there to see me. I feel I've shot out beyond the lighted world, that I'm impersonating myself in a void. How can I be doing these complicated tasks without my mother looking on? How could I have grown up and become the facsimile of a person without her having seen me do it?

IN THE LAST few years, though, something has happened to bring my mother nearer, something like a shift in the temperature of the air around me. She comes back to me not exactly in dreams but in half-visions, in those drowsy times before and after sleeping. In the night, sometimes, she's there, the pieces of her having flown back for a split second to make a hovering presence, like a hologram. I can see her wide smile, the expectancy in her eyes; I get a fleeting sense of her body, of her thick brown hair. Sometimes a whole scene appears: the green forests and blue mountains of New Hampshire, with my mother an eager figure in the foreground, wearing Bermuda shorts and sneakers, ready to climb a mountain.

I'm older now by ten years than my mother was when she died. Time has finally made her the girl and me the fond mother; it's easier now to hold and protect her bright image in my mind. Then, too, my nieces and nephews are growing up, and I can't help watching them through her eyes, even as I'm watching them proudly through my own. They are her grandchildren. Their very presence brings my mother close. My fifteen-year-old niece Alex, Harry's daughter, recently got into a taxi, leaned forward, and gave the driver her address in TriBeCa. My mother would marvel to have a New York granddaughter, not to speak of a New York daughter.

One might say that I'm grieving for her at last, though I'm not really sure what grieving is. Maybe it's just holding still inside and allowing yourself to be inhabited by a strange restlessness. If you can do that, the beloved dead person will sometimes flare into your senses. Sometimes, when I'm in that state of expectant pain, my mother with her sadness and her undying hope flashes across my inner horizon like a lost sensation, like some wonderful music I haven't heard for a long time.

Acknowledgments

THE SOMETIMES SURREAL PROCESS OF WRITING A MEM-
oir puts unusual pressure on the author's friends. I wish to convey
my love and gratitude to Ann Douglas and Stathis Eust, who rescued me in the hardest moments and to whom this book is dedicated, as well as to my other rescuer-supporters, writer Margo
Jefferson, architect and sister-in-law Joan Krevlin, dancer Ulrika
Hallberg.

I also want to thank my family for their thoughtful and sometimes mischievous help in remembering and reconstructing: my
father, Henry Kendall, who responded generously to every phone
call; my brothers who did the same, Judd Esty-Kendall, Harry
Kendall (even if *his* inexplicably happy childhood impaired his
memory), and Sam Kendall; my sister Mardy Kendall who kept
many family details in her memory; my sisters-in-law Cyndy Esty-
Kendall, Cathie Zusy, and again Joan Krevlin; my stepmother

Anita Kendall; my empathetic nieces Alex and Sara Kendall; my late uncle George Conant, and aunt Ellen Conant; my aunts Helen Carothers, Jane Mendelson, and especially Louise Stewart, who read a first draft and encouraged me throughout.

I also want to thank family members for understanding that a family looks different to every person in it—especially my father who is trying now to do a better job of fathering.

I am grateful to my mother's and father's friends and colleagues who helped and supported me at all the stages of remembering (and sometimes became my friends): Anita Bond, Bishop George Cadigan, Charles and Shirley Cason, Bill and Edmee Combs, Denise Dugas, June Dugas, Hedy Epstein, Rumsey and Rosalie Ewing, Frankie Fisher, Ellen Goodman, Teddy Greenbaum, Sally Hasting, Rita Hill, George and Kitty Hoblitzelle, Ruth Jacobson, Ellen Jones, Lois Kaplan, Lee Wilcox Kneerim, Marlene Kopman, Sam Liberman, Rose Mass, Jeff and Dottie Miller, Sally Morse, Millie Muckerman, Charles Oldham, Virginia Hill Robinson, Amey Rodgers, Betsy Roth, Martin Schweig, Dotsie Shapleigh, Edith J. Spink, the Rev. Paul and Fran Smith, Mrs. Sidney Smith, James Sporleder, Beverly Bowen Vickrey, Sinclair and Birchy Weeks, Mrs. Parker Word.

And to my own friends, schoolmates, and colleagues: Michael Anderson, Susan Gillerman Boggs, Mollie Davies, Suzanne Bloom Garment, Donna Schultz Heidbreder, Ronnie Feuerstein Heyman, Marianna Houston-Weber, Michael Lydon, Anne McAlpin, Anna Makkonen, Ellen Mandel, Barry O'Connell, Robert Post, Peggy Dubinsky Price, Joan Rubin, Jane Silverman, Cruce Stark, Kate Thompson, Greig Veeder, Robin Von Breton, David and Jamie Wolf, and my beloved teacher, Michael Gerrard.

Because this memoir also became a social history, I want to thank Aloha and former Aloha people Amy Larson, Carol Radick, Elizabeth B. Smith, and especially Posie Taylor and Nancy Pennell, who have brought Aloha Camp beautifully into the present; Jane Knowles at the Arthur & Elizabeth Schlesinger Library on the History of Women in America; Mrs. Kathie Leavitt at the Reed School; St. Louis filmmaker Curtis Minor; Vassar Summer Institute teacher Eveline Omwake; John Taylor of SLARC; David Laslo at St. Louis Development/CDA; St. Louis civic leaders Percy Green, Kathryn Nelson, Norman Seay, and Margaret Bush Wilson.

Betty Hardin, nurse at the Hayti, Missouri, hospital, responded to my return in 1996 with the same spontaneous generosity she'd offered at the time of the accident in 1969.

Several doctors sustained me during crises: Louis R. DePalo, Norris K. Lee, Lucy Painter, and especially (and imaginatively) Yvonne Porjesz.

Andrea La Sala provided a refuge at her St. Francis Cafe.

My agent, Amanda Urban, offered an astonishing mixture of clear-headedness and faith.

My editor, Kate Medina, my other editor, Meaghan Rady, and my copy editor, Beth Thomas, were true collaborators on this book.

ABOUT THE AUTHOR

ELIZABETH KENDALL is a dance critic
and historian, the author of
Where She Danced: The Birth of American Art-Dance and
*The Runaway Bride: Hollywood Romantic
Comedy of the 1930's.*
She lives in New York City.